San Francisco

YESTERDAY & TODAY ™

J. Kingston Pierce

WEST
SIDE
PUBLISHING

J. Kingston Pierce is a veteran journalist and magazine editor. His previous books include *San Francisco, You're History!, America's Historic Trails with Tom Bodett,* and *Eccentric Seattle.* He has also written for *Salon* and *Travel + Leisure* and was a contributor to the late, lamented *San Francisco Focus* magazine. He lives in Seattle.

Charles Fracchia is a native San Franciscan and founder and president emeritus of the San Francisco Museum and Historical Society. He is the author of 12 books, including *Fire and Gold: The San Francisco Story* and *City by the Bay: A History of San Francisco 1945 to the Present.* He teaches at the University of San Francisco and City College of San Francisco.

Robert Holmes is a photographer who has traveled the world for major magazines, including *National Geographic, Travel Holiday, Life, Time, Travel + Leisure, GEO,* and *Islands.* He was the first person to twice receive the Travel Photographer of the Year Award from the Society of American Travel Writers. You can learn more about Holmes at www.robertholmesphotography.com.

Yesterday & Today is a trademark of Publications International, Ltd.

West Side Publishing is a division of Publications International, Ltd.

Louis Weber, CEO
Publications International, Ltd.
7373 North Cicero Avenue
Lincolnwood, Illinois 60712

ISBN-13: 978-1-4127-1575-1
ISBN-10: 1-4127-1575-X

Manufactured in China.

8 7 6 5 4 3 2 1

Library of Congress Control Number: 2008931661

The tallest and arguably the most recognizable edifice in San Francisco, the Transamerica Pyramid glows amid the other Financial District towers at dusk.

Contents

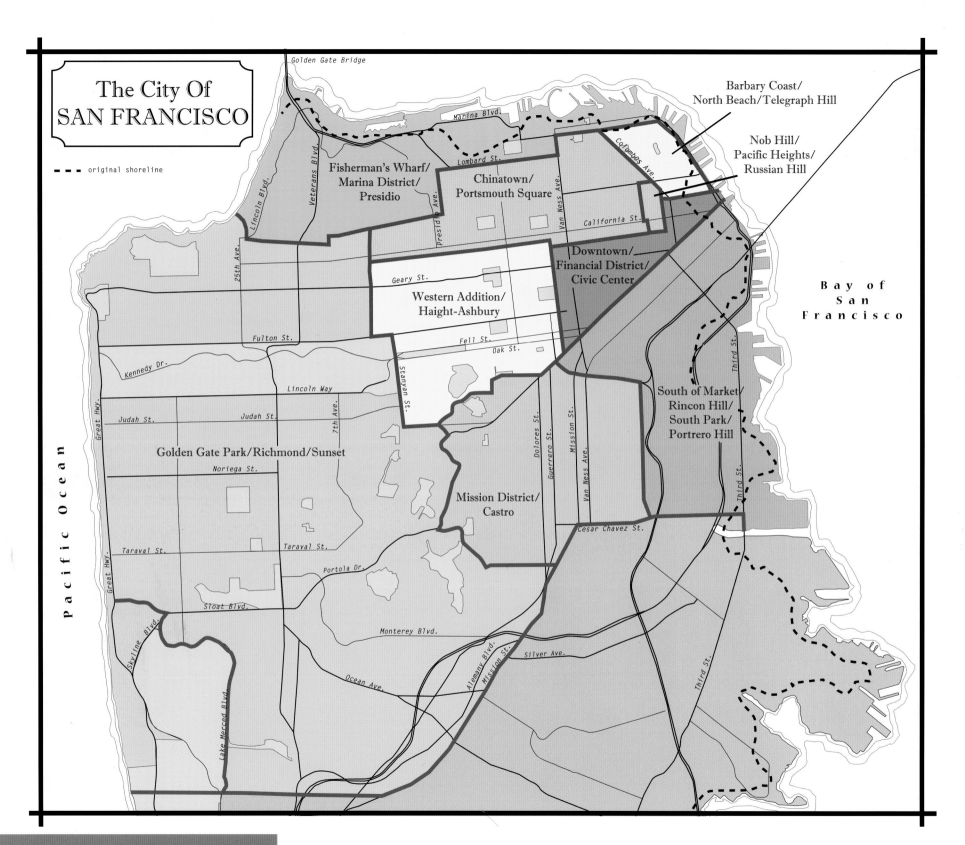

The City Of
SAN FRANCISCO

- - - original shoreline

Golden Gate Bridge

Barbary Coast/
North Beach/Telegraph Hill

Nob Hill/
Pacific Heights/
Russian Hill

Fisherman's Wharf/
Marina District/
Presidio

Chinatown/
Portsmouth Square

Downtown/
Financial District/
Civic Center

Western Addition/
Haight-Ashbury

South of Market/
Rincon Hill/
South Park/
Portrero Hill

Golden Gate Park/Richmond/Sunset

Mission District/
Castro

Pacific Ocean

Bay of
San
Francisco

Marina Blvd.
Lombard St.
Columbus Ave.
Van Ness Ave.
California St.
Veterans Blvd.
Lincoln Blvd.
Presidio Ave.
25th Ave.
Geary St.
Fulton St.
Fell St.
Oak St.
Stanyan St.
Kennedy Dr.
Lincoln Way
Judah St.
Judah St.
7th Ave.
Noriega St.
Taraval St.
Taraval St.
Portola Dr.
Great Hwy.
Great Hwy.
Sloat Blvd.
Skyline Blvd.
Lake Merced Blvd.
Monterey Blvd.
Ocean Ave.
Alemany Blvd.
Mission St.
Silver Ave.
Cesar Chavez St.
Dolores St.
Guerrero St.
Mission St.
Van Ness Ave.
Third St.
Third St.

"America's Last Great Metropolitan Village"

Opinions on San Francisco have varied wildly over the last century and a half. During his return to England after a trip to Australia in 1875, Victorian novelist Anthony Trollope stopped over in the Bay Area just long enough to determine that "There is almost nothing to see in San Francisco that is worth seeing." Even journalist and *Devil's Dictionary* creator Ambrose Bierce, whose acidic "prattlings" decorated pages of the local press during much of the late 19th century, called this city a "paradise of ignorance, anarchy, and general yellowness."

On the other hand, Fresno-born author William Saroyan declared San Francisco "the genius of American cities." English writer and poet Rudyard Kipling applauded it in its gawky, Gilded Age adolescence as "a mad city—inhabited for the most part by perfectly insane people whose women are of a remarkable beauty."

And Jack Kerouac, who ventured out here from the East Coast in the 1950s to hang with the Beats, left with rosy memories of "the wine, the alleys, the poorboys, Third Street, poets, painters, Buddhists, bums, junkies, girls, millionaires, MGs, the whole fabulous movie of San Francisco...the tug at your heart." Novelist-essayist Herbert Gold once called San Francisco "America's last great metropolitan village. It is a place to be explained, like a blind man defining an elephant—different wherever you happen to touch it." Even natives may be familiar with only parts of its hide, while the impression of visitors is shaped by their expectations—and after 150 years of this town being flattered, flogged, and photographed, there's almost no way anyone can come here without expectations and preconceived notions.

This, after all, is the city of Dashiell Hammett and *The Maltese Falcon*, Armistead Maupin and *Tales of the City*, Amy Tan and *The Joy Luck Club*. It's the city of *Barbary Coast* and *Bullitt*, *Dirty Harry* and *Mrs. Doubtfire*. It's the city

This 1850 daguerreotype, one of the earlist known photographic processes, is said to be the oldest snapshot of San Francisco.

A panoramic view of sprawling San Francisco today uncovers downtown skyscrapers, the Bay Bridge, and Alcatraz Island in the foggy distance.

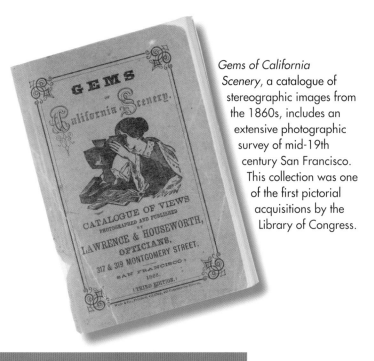

Gems of California Scenery, a catalogue of stereographic images from the 1860s, includes an extensive photographic survey of mid-19th century San Francisco. This collection was one of the first pictorial acquisitions by the Library of Congress.

of *Have Gun, Will Travel* and *Ironside, Dharma & Greg* and *McMillan & Wife*, and of course, *The Streets of San Francisco*.

It's the city of soaring bridges and sourdough bread. It's the city where people should be sure to wear flowers in their hair, where Tony Bennett left his heart, and where Mark Twain got his big break. It's columnist Herb Caen's Baghdad-by-the-Bay and President William Howard Taft's "The City That Knows How." It's a place that, even at its humblest, even after being leveled by earthquakes and siroccos of flame, can still impress.

"Our fair city lies in ruins," Mayor Eugene Schmitz said after San Francisco was reduced to a malodorous cinder in 1906, "but those are the damndest finest ruins ever seen on the face of the earth."

It is a spot proud of its place in the world—The City, as residents like to call it, as if no other municipality could challenge its stature, splendor, and sophistication. And few do, which is why San Francisco is now one of the most visited cities in the world.

Take that, Mr. Trollope.

Buckets of bouquets and afternoon strollers sprinkled the sidewalks in the 1970s, as an overflowing cable car takes passengers past the corner of Powell and Geary streets.

SAN FRANCISCO.

From Gold to Ashes

Were residents of mid-19th century San Francisco transported to the downtown of today, they wouldn't recognize the cloud-tickling towers or most of the wide thoroughfares that crisscross this urban hive. They'd stand in absolute terror before the ceaseless bustle that keeps this city running. But they would certainly recognize the combination of confidence, ambition, and stubborn determination that makes all of this craziness possible. Those same human drives—amped by a dash of greed—were what first lifted San Francisco from the sandy, windblown peninsula it now inarguably dominates.

The seed of this town was planted as one of three ingredients of Spanish colonial occupation. On the shoreline just east of the Golden Gate rose the first of those components: the Presidio, a modest military installation founded in 1776—the same year the United States declared its independence from Great Britain—as the northernmost reminder of Spain's empire in North America. Dedicated shortly thereafter but located three miles inland to the southeast was La Misión de San Francisco de Asís—better known as Mission Dolores—which was built and operated by Franciscan missionaries from Mexico determined to "civilize" the Ohlone Indians who had been living peacefully along the mid-California coast for hundreds of years. In between those poles of peninsular settlement sprouted the pueblo of Yerba Buena, named after a local mint-flavored plant from which the Native Americans and the Spanish brewed tea.

THE RUSH BEGINS

Development was slow initially, though it was helped by Mexico's decision to break free of Spanish rule in 1821 and allow increased commercial trade with New England ports. But the pace of growth quickened after 1846, when during the Mexican-American War a contingent of sailors from the warship *Portsmouth* rowed ashore and liberated Yerba Buena for the United States. A year later, the ambitious young hamlet ditched its original moniker and adopted the name of the mammoth San Francisco Bay beside which it sat.

In 1849, after gold was discovered to the east, San Francisco swelled in a mad rush. Some 300,000 people poured into the town over the next six years, bound for the goldfields around German émigré John Sutter's sawmill on the American River. Their arrival spurred the creation of saloons, new hotels, gambling "hells,"

Hundreds of thousands of people from around the country charged to San Francisco to get a share of the gold discovered in the Sierra Nevada foothills.

Left: A hand-colored impression of San Francisco. The view is from a hilltop, looking toward the Bay, circa 1850.

brothels, banks, and other businesses considered essential in a city dominated by young men with too much wealth in their pockets. Yerba Buena Cove, in which so many ships had arrived during the gold rush, was eventually filled with dirt and sand from Telegraph Hill, increasing the size of the Financial District. And more trappings of a permanent habitation took root. French restaurants opened, as did theaters and bookstores, and newspapers began rolling off clamorous printing presses. Streetcar lines were extended west from downtown to new residential districts, and Andrew Hallidie's cable cars increased property values on nearby Nob Hill. But growth often outdistanced refinement. Unpaved roadways became hazards in heavy rains, and horses were said to disappear beneath the mud. Garbage was simply dumped into the streets, and during the summer months, blowing sand and dry dirt blinded a growing number of women on their way to the City of Paris department store.

PROSPERITY ON THE COAST

It wasn't until the late 1890s, after the gold rush and a second wave of riches had poured in—this one from silver strikes around Virginia City, Nevada—that reformers began harnessing private affluence for public improvements. Despite national economic downturns, the city was prospering thanks to the mining of natural resources, commercial shipping, and manufacturing. Folks such as Mayor James D. Phelan, a progressive inspired by the romantic grandeur of Chicago's 1893 World's Fair and the "city beautiful movement" that it birthed, wanted to use community tax revenues to re-create San Francisco as a "Paris of the Pacific," supplanting what remained of its frontier shabbiness with grand boulevards, museums, and municipal greenswards on the order of Golden Gate Park, which at the time was still under construction.

The city's earthquake and fire of April 1906 might have been seen as a rare opportunity by civic reformers, for it razed more than 28,000 buildings over an area of 4.7 square miles, leaving downtown San Francisco a largely blank slate ripe for an aesthetic reawakening. Unfortunately, merchants and pragmatic officials decided it was more important to rebuild downtown *quickly* rather than *well*. And so they set aside a richly landscaped and pedestrian-friendly comprehensive plan that had already been envisioned by architect Daniel H. Burnham, the chief of construction for the 1893 Chicago Exposition, and got down to the work of reconstruction—this time using more brick and stone than wood. Urban enhancement, declared the *San Francisco Bulletin*, would have to be left to a "future and more opulent generation."

PRESERVE & RESTORE

Actually, several subsequent generations have engineered such downtown improvements: building a classical-style Civic Center to showcase government and culture; preserving and restoring architectural landmarks, even amid pressures to tear down and build anew; saving the last of the clanking cable cars—familiar symbols of this hilly metropolis—from being "modernized" out of existence; and reconceiving the Embarcadero as a public esplanade after a 1989 earthquake required the destruction of an elevated freeway that for too long had cut off downtown from waterfront views.

Sometimes ambition isn't such a bad thing in a city.

Traffic bustles down Market Street, circa 1892.

An aerial view of downtown San Francisco today

THE FERRY BUILDING

Until the Golden Gate Bridge and the San Francisco-Oakland Bay Bridge were constructed in the 1930s, ferries were a transportation necessity. In 1875, a wooden Ferry House was built at the northeast end of Market Street, on what is now the Embarcadero. Unless one ventured northward along the peninsula, ferries or other boats once provided the only means of reaching San Francisco. They were also the fastest way out, as San Franciscans knew well in 1906, when thousands of refugees fled before the fire engulfing their city. Mobs rushed to the Ferry Building, begging for passage to Oakland and Alameda *(left)*.

By the time of the earthquake and fire, though, it was a new, larger ferry terminal that greeted passengers. Opened in 1898, it welcomed 50 million people every year, making it second only to London's Charing Cross Station as a busy transportation crossroads. Boats landed at the docks there about 170 times a day, and trolley lines sped away from the waterfront landmark every 20 seconds.

But beginning in the 1930s, ferry ridership sharply declined, and by the 1950s, the Ferry Building was in scant use. Its once grand interior was subdivided into offices, and archways and mosaic floors were trashed. In the early 21st century, however, the long neglected landmark was restored as much as possible to its 1898 splendor. It is mainly an upscale marketplace now, the skylit interior filled with gourmet shops and restaurants. The building was also rededicated as a ferry terminal.

The Ferry Building has attracted the attention of more than just ferry passengers. Its position at Market Street and the Embarcadero has made it a familiar sight for drivers, bike enthusiasts, and streetcar riders. (Below, a Geary streetcar loads passengers in front of the terminal in 1934.) Today, locals and tourists converge on the popular farmers market set up in front of the building twice a week, and during warm weather office workers from surrounding skyscrapers gather for lunch in adjacent Justin Herman Plaza.

Architect A. Page Brown was generally responsible for the Ferry Building's design. A New Yorker who had worked for the distinguished Eastern firm of McKim, Mead and White before moving to California, Brown patterned his Union Depot and Ferry House after a railroad station developed for Chicago's 1893 World's Columbian Exposition. He took his inspiration for the clock tower from the 12th-century Giralda bell tower on the Cathedral of Seville in Spain, as well as from the bell tower of St. Mark's Basilica in Venice, Italy.

Cars travel south on the one-way Montgomery Street, May 6, 1947.

FINANCIAL DISTRICT

Before the California gold rush, Montgomery Street was a poor excuse for a thoroughfare, clinging to the edge of Yerba Buena Cove. It was advertised by merchants as "Montgomery Street on the Beach," as if that would somehow make its windblown sandlots, pine-board shacks, and musty barrooms more fashionable. It didn't. However, the discovery of gold at Sutter's Mill finally brought a shine to this road, along which sprouted brokerage houses, auction shops, and shipping offices. By the 1860s, Montgomery was the town's main business street. It has since become a canyon of commerce; its bordering towers—including the Mills Building, the city's oldest example of Chicago skyscraper design (created by Windy City architect Daniel H. Burnham in 1891), and the taller Russ Building, a 1927 neo-Gothic high-rise that takes its cues from Chicago's Tribune Tower—are tall enough to block out the sun by early afternoon. Even more than a century and a half after the gold rush, Montgomery Street remains the center of San Francisco's Financial District.

Montgomery Street today. Shown here on each side of the buzzing traffic are the Russ Building (left) and the Mills Building (right).

MADMAN OF THE PEOPLE

Joshua Abraham Norton is said to have arrived in San Francisco in 1849, and he grew rich off real-estate investments and commodities trading. But after losing a fortune in 1852, Norton disappeared. He returned eight years later, wearing a militarylike uniform and calling himself Norton I, Emperor of the United States and Protector of Mexico.

Norton I, Emperor

Norton's business failure may have unbalanced his mind, or maybe he was just an uncanny actor and con man. In either event, he was awarded 20 years of the most bizarre respect ever shown to an American. He'd walk through the streets, greet people as if they were his loyal subjects, and receive salutes in return. He regularly attended legislative sessions in Sacramento and counseled lawmakers. He ate for free at restaurants, and theaters loyally reserved three seats for him and his two dogs. On the rare occasions when Norton actually needed money, he had promissory notes printed, and amazingly, people accepted them.

San Franciscans saw Emperor Norton as the embodiment of their young city's charming, offbeat character and loved him for it. After he died suddenly on January 8, 1880, the city buried Norton with all the pomp and circumstance befitting a crowned head of state, and about 30,000 people showed up for his funeral.

Although Montgomery has a history of catering to buttoned-down moneylenders, briefcase-wielding businessmen, and the numerous office workers who keep their enterprises bustling, it's also a street to which famous personalities wanting some attention—and perhaps financial backing, as well—have taken their causes or have done "victory laps." *Above:* A grinning President Harry S. Truman waves his hat to welcoming crowds during a visit to the city in June 1945, shortly before the end of World War II.

San Francisco Stock and Bond Exchange

Local capitalists founded the San Francisco Stock and Bond Exchange in 1882 at 312 California Street. In 1930, it was relocated to what had been a U.S. Sub-Treasury building at Sansome and Pine streets *(left)*, and an office tower was erected adjacent to it. The trading floor was located in the multipillared, classical-style building that had been the Sub-Treasury. In 2002, the trading floor was closed, and stock trading went electronic. Four years later, the company that owned the Pacific Exchange was bought out by the New York Stock Exchange, which ended operations under the previous name.

The two monumental granite sculptures flanking the entrance to the old Pacific Exchange are the work of Ralph Stackpole, an Oregon-born artist who studied at the California School of Fine Arts and the École des Beaux-Arts in Paris. The sculpture shown here is called *Man's Inventive Genius* and features male figures. Its mate, *Earth's Fulfillness,* features female figures.

Wells Fargo Bank

The Financial District hosted the earliest headquarters of Wells, Fargo & Co., with its first modest office opening in 1852 *(inset)*. It still maintains its corporate headquarters on Montgomery Street *(left)*, but it's better known for its 1910 Beaux Arts–style building at Grant and Market streets (above, in the 1950s). Decorated inside with white and green marbles, the structure was designed by Clinton Day, a local architect who was also responsible for downtown's once beloved City of Paris department store.

TRANSAMERICA BUILDING AND THE "MONKEY BLOCK"

When it first went up in the early 1970s, the Transamerica Pyramid—the loftiest and by now the most familiar spire adorning the San Francisco cityscape at 853 feet—provoked a torrent of controversy. Locals who disapproved of the pyramid were more than happy to mention that it had been designed by a firm from rival Los Angeles, William Pereira and Associates. No longer home to the Transamerica Corporation, the building has grown on San Franciscans over time.

Some, though, still miss the historic building that once occupied this site: the Montgomery Block, otherwise known as the "Monkey Block." Built in 1853, at the behest of Henry Wager Halleck, a prosperous lawyer and land developer who would later serve as a Union Army commander during the Civil War, the Monkey Block was designed in the Italianate style by Philadelphia architect Gordon P. Cummings. The four-story building was known for its restaurants and for its studios and apartments occupied by artists and writers. Mark Twain, Ambrose Bierce, Robert Louis Stevenson, and Jack London are all said to have rented there.

Despite its heritage as a bohemian landmark, the Monkey Block was torn down in 1959, just as the architectural preservation movement was beginning to take hold in San Francisco.

The historic Montgomery Block, or "Monkey Block," is shown here in 1956.

Hallidie Building

More roundly loved than the Transamerica Pyramid is the Hallidie Building. The work of Willis Polk, an architectural disciple of Daniel H. Burnham, the Hallidie was erected in 1917 for the University of California. It was named after one of its regents, Andrew S. Hallidie, who had developed San Francisco's cable cars. It's a novel structure and an early example of the sort of glass curtain wall construction that would become a signature of 20th-century modernist architecture. The American Institute of Architects has its San Francisco chapter in the Hallidie Building. (*Above left:* The Hallidie Building, circa 1920s–30s. *Above right:* The Hallidie Building today.)

DOWNTOWN HOTELS

San Francisco has always been a travelers' town, rampant with hotels. That goes back to the 1840s, when people returned from the goldfields, exhausted and in serious need of a bath and a good night's sleep. It's said that the first public lodging here was the City Hotel at the corner of Clay and Kearny streets.

By the 1860s, hotels were becoming bigger and grander. The Russ House, filling an entire block of Montgomery Street, boasted a restaurant, ballroom, and a luxurious jewelry store done in marble and glass. Also on Montgomery was the Lick House. Created by James Lick, a Pennsylvania cabinetmaker who'd grown rich off early San Francisco real-estate purchases and farming in the Santa Clara Valley, the hotel featured a dining room that imitated one in France's Palace of Versailles, but with mirrors and murals of California landscapes along its walls. Then there was the impressive Baldwin Hotel *(right)*, a French Renaissance–style building wrapping around the corner of Market and Powell streets. Constructed by Comstock millionaire Elias Jackson "Lucky" Baldwin, this hotel had its own luxury theater, a 168-foot-tall dome topping a five-story courtyard, and the well-known $25,000 Tiffany lobby clock. Of that timepiece, Mark Twain said it told "not only the hours, minutes and seconds, but the turn of the tides, the phases of the moon, the price of eggs and who's got your umbrella."

A meal ticket for breakfast at the Baldwin Hotel

A menu from President William McKinley's banquet at the Palace Hotel in 1901

THE PALACE HOTEL

No local lodgings of the 19th century compared to the Palace Hotel. Opened on Market Street at New Montgomery in 1875, it was the creation of ambitious banker William C. Ralston. For a few years, the Palace was the largest and most deluxe hotel in the United States. It was seven stories tall and covered 2.5 acres with more than 750 guest rooms, a quartet of oversize, redwood-paneled elevators ("rising rooms," they were called at the time), a crystal roof garden, a kitchen big enough to serve 1,200 guests, and a facade ribboned by banks of bay windows with views of downtown.

The Palace had even been constructed in defense against natural catastrophes. Its outer walls were two feet thick and double strips of iron reinforced them at four-foot intervals. Tucked into the building's subbasement was a reservoir holding 630,000 gallons of water. Ralston had installed rudimentary electric fire detectors in every room and scheduled hallway patrols at 30-minute intervals day and night. The supposition was that if the rest of San Francisco burned to a crisp, the Palace would endure. That proved erroneous: The hotel was gutted during the 1906 fire.

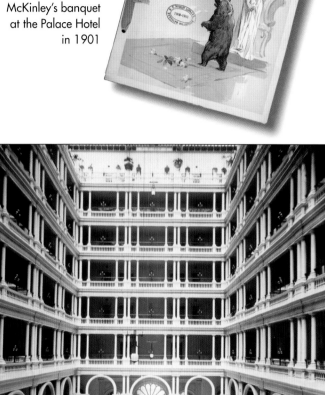

The original Palace Hotel strove to be opulent in every respect. The open, seven-story, skylit center of the building known as the Grand Court served as a carriage entrance for dignitaries and other deep-pocketed visitors to the city. It was here in 1879 that Union Army General and former President Ulysses S. Grant greeted crowds of well-wishers after stopping in the city on the final leg of an around-the-world tour.

A throng gathers on O'Farrell Street to watch the fire lick its way west along Market Street toward the Call Building, consuming everything in its path.

1906 EARTHQUAKE AND FIRE

Events are often said to forever change things, but at least in the case of San Francisco's 1906 earthquake and fire, there's no doubt about its impact. The devastation commenced offshore just after 5 A.M. on April 18, when the earth ruptured along California's 296-mile San Andreas Fault with a force equal to 15 million tons of TNT. Forests of mighty redwoods were toppled like toothpicks. Ships 150 miles out in the Pacific Ocean were jolted, their captains convinced that they had somehow struck a reef or sunken wreckage. Fort Bragg, a blue-collar town on the Mendocino Coast, jiggled and collapsed.

At just after 5:12 A.M., 20 minutes before dawn, the shock pummeled San Francisco. There were two principal tremors, each lasting less than a minute, with dozens of aftershocks continuing into the next day. The Richter magnitude scale hadn't yet been developed in 1906, but estimates since then have rated it at a magnitude of 7.8 on a scale of 1 to 10, down from an original estimate of 8.3. The quake sent "earth waves" two to three feet high roaring through the ground, threatening the foundations of even the mightiest buildings. Streetcar tracks reared from their bolts and bent around like angry vipers. Long, jagged tears opened the middles of concrete streets. Water gushed from broken lines. Gas spit up from openings in the sidewalk. The facade of City Hall, finished only six years before, peeled away until all that remained was the cagework beneath. What remained of gaslights fighting the darkness went out immediately. Horses, spooked by the commotion of sparks thrown from severed power lines and people screaming all around them, broke their tethers and stampeded through downtown, joining platoons of rats already running for their pitiful lives.

And then the *real* devastation began.

Over the next three days, fires erupting all over town did the most damage. Half an hour after the earth stopped shaking, the city was engulfed in clouds of smoke five miles high. Efforts to create firebreaks by dynamiting buildings in the fire's path more often spread the calamity further. Onlookers in adjacent Oakland and Berkeley were convinced that San Francisco was being wiped off the map.

COPYR

THE 1906 AFTERMATH

The 1906 earthquake had been bad enough, but the fire that followed was twice the size of the one that flattened Chicago in 1871. It destroyed more than 28,000 buildings over an area of 4.7 square miles—three-quarters of the city. Some 225,000 San Franciscans—more than half of the city's entire population—were left homeless by the disaster. Many of them retreated to Golden Gate Park and the Presidio, where they established tent cities so they at least had somewhere to sleep. Having abandoned their residences, people were left to start over, shopping impromptu stores on Market Street *(above)*.

Estimates of the numbers killed in San Francisco's earthquake and fire have varied from 478—a low count in the immediate aftermath of the catastrophe—to 6,000. Something closer to 3,000 is more likely. Everywhere, there was a sense that the city would never be the same. Yet expectation was in the air. "The great calamity... left no one with the impression that it amounted to an irrevocable loss," English writer H. G. Wells explained years later in *The Future in America: A Search After Realities*. "Nowhere is there any doubt but that San Francisco will rise again, bigger, better, and soon."

And so it did.

Quake Heard 'Round the World

Newspapers spread word of the unfolding disaster across the nation. The Utica, New York *Herald-Dispatch* headlined, "City of San Francisco Now Only a Blackened Ruin." Americans were transfixed by the Bay Area tragedy. *Above:* Capitalizing on the debacle, the Michaelis Publishing Company of Kansas City, Missouri, produced a booklet called *Ruins of San Francisco,* filled with black and white photographs of the wreckage.

Looking southwest on Market Street from the Ferry Building, downtown appeared to have been carpet bombed.

Lotta's Fountain, 1885

LOTTA'S FOUNTAIN

Lotta's Fountain is the oldest surviving monument in San Francisco. Protruding from the often windy intersection of Market, Geary, and Kearny streets, this landmark was dedicated on September 9, 1875—the 25th anniversary of California's admission into the Union—and was a gift from Charlotte Mignon "Lotta" Crabtree. A vivacious, redheaded entertainer, Crabtree was born in New York City and arrived in primitive San Francisco in 1853 at age six. Crabtree, fondly known as "the California Diamond," soon enchanted Americans, but she never forgot the place that had helped make her a child star. And so in 1875, when Crabtree was famous and wealthy, she had a fancy, cast-iron drinking fountain made and dedicated it to the city.

San Franciscans came to appreciate Lotta's Fountain after the 1906 earthquake and fire. While the grand edifices surrounding it were destroyed, the rococo fountain came through the debacle virtually unscathed. It became a rallying point for survivors, and it was there, too, that the names of the dead were posted. Ever since, the dwindling ranks of earthquake survivors gather in remembrance on April 18, at 5:12 A.M., along with other San Franciscans paying tribute to their city's spirit.

Irma Allred and Elma Hammer give Crabtree's eccentric legacy in cast iron a conscientious cleaning during the early 1900s. Note the lions' heads on all four corners of the fountain and the basins served by spigots in the shape of griffins' heads.

To celebrate the fountain's repair, Chief Administrative Officer Tom Mellon and City Supervisor (later U.S. Senator) Dianne Feinstein shared the first mugs of drinking water from the renovated landmark's spigots on August 20, 1974 (above). Two decades later and after years of complaints about the fountain being dirty and disregarded, it was temporarily removed, refurbished again at a cost of $160,000, cut down to its original size (after growing by eight feet in 1916 to match the height of new street lamps along Market), and rededicated in the late 1990s.

Although it has survived for more than a century, Lotta's Fountain has not done so unchanged. Gone are the tin cups that originally dangled from its quartet of semicircular fountain basins. Added was a bronze relief plaque in 1911, commemorating a concert from the year before given by Italian soprano Luisa Tetrazzini, who sang at Lotta's Fountain before a crowd of 250,000 people to celebrate the city's reemergence from its ashes.

NEWSPAPER CROSSROADS

Outside Montgomery Street, perhaps the most prestigious address in downtown San Francisco in 1900 was the intersection of Third and Market streets. This crossroads was called the "Newspaper Angle," thanks to its concentration of buildings housing the city's biggest daily papers. The most significant of these constructions was the *San Francisco Chronicle* headquarters, opened in 1890 and designed for publisher Michael H. de Young by Chicago architects Daniel H. Burnham and John Wellborn Root. Distinguished by its grandiose and intricately carved entry archway and four-story clock tower, the Chronicle Building was San Francisco's first high-rise.

Although the newspaper claimed that its clifflike, Romanesque headquarters (shown at right in 1904) was the "safest, strongest, and in every way one of the finest office buildings in the world," an accident in 1905 proved its vulnerability. A parade celebrating the reelection of Mayor Eugene Schmitz—whom the paper had opposed—halted outside the Chronicle Building to blast off a few skyrockets. This in-your-face gesture went wrong, though, when the rockets set the clock tower on fire. Afterward, de Young added two stories to his edifice, but he did not replace the timepiece.

Not to be outshone by de Young, Claus Spreckels—sugar mogul and owner of the rival *San Francisco Call*—commissioned architects James and Merritt Reid to create a home for his paper on the corner of Third, Market, and Kearny in the late 1890s. The 18-story Call Building had a classical entrance and a heavily embellished dome anchored by turrets *(left)*.

The *Chronicle* tower *(foreground)* was seriously damaged in the 1906 fire, and the newspaper relocated to its current home at Fifth and Mission streets in 1924. Its original headquarters was left to be allocated as office space. Not until the early 21st century was this de Young Building largely restored—though a 24-story condominium tower was clapped to its back.

The *San Francisco Sentinal (inset)* was one of the first African-American newspapers in the West.

Unfortunately, all the Sugar King's influence couldn't save the Call Building in 1906. Fire from the adjacent San Francisco Gas & Electric Company plant was sucked up the elevator shaft of Spreckels's pride and joy, causing the tower to burn. The *Call* headquarters was rebuilt but lost its elegant dome in 1938 to make room for six additional stories. It's now known as the Central Building *(right)*.

The Hearst Building

Completing the "Newspaper Angle" was the headquarters of William Randolph Hearst's *San Francisco Examiner*. Hearst's father had acquired the *Examiner* in 1880. Seven years later, he reluctantly turned it over to his ambitious 23-year-old son, who in turn proceeded to make the *Examiner* the foundation of his American newspaper empire. In the early 1890s, the younger Hearst commissioned Albert C. Schweinfurth to develop an impressive new headquarters for the *Examiner (left)*. Like so many other downtown structures, though, it succumbed to the 1906 fire. The Hearst Building was rebuilt and the *Examiner* became the city's most influential newspaper in the 1920s and '30s. *Above:* The Hearst Building today, showing its decorative facade designed in 1937 (along with other renovations) by architect Julia Morgan.

POWELL AND MARKET CABLE CARS

Cable cars have been running north along Powell Street since the 1880s, carrying locals from downtown up and over Nob and Russian hills. In recent years, the cable cars have transported tourists to Fisherman's Wharf and Aquatic Park near Ghirardelli Square. On sunny summer days, you're lucky *not* to find a long line of people waiting for a ride at the intersection of Powell and Market streets. It's there, in the broad-shouldered shadow of the Flood Building (shown on the far right in 1953), that a wooden turntable transforms southbound cable cars into northbound ones. Once replenished with passengers, the historic, single-ended cars resume their clanking, brake-screeching, and bell-ringing climb past Union Square, Victorian row houses, venerable apartment buildings, restaurants, and a Cable Car Museum that celebrates this city's distinctive transportation heritage.

UNION SQUARE

In 1847, Jasper O'Farrell, the Irish-born surveyor, revamped and greatly expanded an earlier survey for a budding Yerba Buena—in the process giving San Francisco its broad, diagonal Market Street—and designated what's now Union Square as open space. It took several years for the park to be laid out on what had been a sandy hillslope, which was given to the town by John W. Geary, a hero of the Mexican-American War. The square, bounded by Geary, Powell, Post, and Stockton streets, was named during the Civil War in honor of pro-Union rallies held there.

Above: In 1903, the 95-foot-tall memorial at the center of this plaza was erected to commemorate U.S. Admiral George Dewey's victory during the 1898 Battle of Manila Bay. The bronze figure of a voluptuous woman—*Victory*—atop the granite column was modeled on Alma de Bretteville, a celebrity belle who would go on to wed the son of sugar and newspaper magnate Claus Spreckels. The plaza and memorial are pictured in the 1920s–'30s.

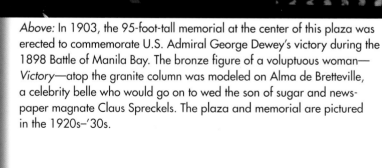

Union Square today on a sunny afternoon

During the 1906 disaster, Union Square became a rallying point for refugees. It soon emerged as the nexus of San Francisco's foremost shopping and hotel district. In the early 1940s, it was redesigned to accommodate a then novel underground parking garage. In 2002, after years of the park's decline followed by a $25 million renovation, the 2.6-acre square reopened. Along with its promenade and stage, the plaza features heart-shape sculpures created by local artists and celebrities. *Inset:* One of the heart sculptures bears an image of the Golden Gate Bridge, painted by veteran crooner Tony Bennett. Bennett's signature song, of course, is "I Left My Heart in San Francisco."

THE PARIS LEAVES SAN FRANCISCO

THE NEIMAN MARCUS STORE at Union Square sits on a spot once occupied by the City of Paris, a popular emporium and department store.

It was founded in 1850 by brothers Felix and Emile Verdier, who traveled here from Nîmes, France. They opened their first shop on Portsmouth Square, and in the mid-1890s, the City of Paris moved to Union Square. Though entirely hollowed out by the 1906 fire, the establishment was one of the few to survive the catastrophe. It was restored two years later by architect Arthur Brown, Jr., and embellished with a four-story rotunda, prominent for its art-nouveau skylight by Harry Wile Hopps.

The City of Paris remained a local institution until the 1970s, when upscale retailer Neiman Marcus announced it would replace the store with one of its own. The new building, designed by Philip Johnson and John Burgee, retained only the City of Paris's rotunda and glass dome.

MAIDEN LANE

Dividing the block of Stockton Street between Post and Geary streets, you'll find a shady, pleasant alleyway called Maiden Lane. Today, it caters to shoppers, lunchtime diners, and visitors to the Circle Gallery Building, a significant Frank Lloyd Wright creation. But a century ago, this place was known as Morton Street and was bordered by some of the city's busiest houses of prostitution. Although located outside San Francisco's bawdy quarter, these types of businesses along Morton Street profited for more than 40 years. During daylight hours when business was slower, women reclined in casement windows wearing nothing from the waist up. There wasn't anything subtle about the trade transacted here, but policemen generally turned a blind eye to the goings-on.

Outraged ladies' groups and religious crusaders tried many times to shut down Morton Street, as did the San Francisco Board of Supervisors, which officially banned the use of buildings there for prostitution in the early 1890s. However, it took the 1906 earthquake and fire to permanently extinguish Morton Street's red lights.

The "Spring Comes to Maiden Lane" festival (shown above on April 10, 1947) was once held annually by the Maiden Lane Merchants Association.

Quaint cafés and shops occupy most of Maiden Lane today.

MARKET STREET SHOPPING

Major landowners were so incensed by surveyor Jasper O'Farrell's 1847 proposal to cut a grand, 120-foot-wide boulevard diagonally through central San Francisco that they threatened to lynch the Irishman. Over the century and a half since, this thoroughfare has been a travel corridor and an essential artery of this city's life. Comparing it to Paris's Champs-Élysées is hardly an original thought anymore. Market has played host to everything from parades, riots, and locals fleeing the 1906 disaster to hagglers, highbinders, beggars, moguls, and presidents. Dignitaries traveled along here in 1945 on their way to the Civic Center to create the United Nations.

The Burnett Bros. Jewelry Store and its sidewalk clock became nationally known in 1916 following a suitcase-bomb explosion near the Ferry Building in the midst of a giant Preparedness Day parade, held in anticipation of America's entry into World War I. Ten spectators were killed and another 40 were wounded. A pair of "radical" labor leaders were charged with causing the carnage. However, a photograph showing one of them in front of the Burnett Bros. sidewalk clock—blocks away—at the time of the detonation raised questions. Regardless, death sentences were handed down for both men. Their punishments were later commuted to life imprisonment and both were eventually pardoned. The photo here shows the "Alibi Clock" in the 1920s. In the early '30s, it was relocated to the sidewalk in front of a jeweler's shop in the Bay Area town of Vallejo.

Appropriate to its name, Market has always bustled with shoppers. Browsers study the blooms at a Market flower stand in 1945.

CIVIC CENTER

San Francisco's City Hall started out on the edge of Portsmouth Square, where in 1852 the Jenny Lind Theater was transformed into the center of local government. In 1870, though, the Board of Supervisors—hoping to boost real-estate values—chose to relocate City Hall to the triangle outlined by Market, Larkin, and McAllister streets, formerly occupied by a city cemetery. Canadian architects Augustus Laver and Thomas Fuller secured the contract to design the structure, but building their grandiose Second Empire structure *(top right)* proved too costly. Instead, a committee of local architects assumed the task of creating a civic center, which took 24 years to build and was dominated by a disproportionately tall City Hall dome. Only a few years later, the 1906 earthquake stripped City Hall of its facade, leaving only the frame beneath. The once elegant dome resembled a birdcage *(bottom right)*.

After efforts to incorporate a new government center into a comprehensive replanning of San Francisco failed, promoters saw an opportunity in Congress's proposal to hold a national exposition celebrating the opening of the Panama Canal. Boosters wanted to hold the fair in San Francisco as a way to announce that the fire-ravaged city was back in business, and they viewed a new city hall important in driving that message home. Integral to these projects was James "Sunny Jim" Rolph, Jr., a shipbuilder and bank executive who moved into the mayor's office in 1912 and set about raising public funds for the construction endeavor.

THE ORIGINAL DESIGN
FOR THE
NEW CITY HALL AND LAW COURTS.
SAN FRANCISCO CAL

P.H.CANAVAN Esq
Chairman   Board
J.G.EASTLAND Esq   City Hall Commiss'rs
C.E.McLANE Esq

FULLER & LAVER
Architects
ROBERT GEORGE
Ass't to the Board

The original design for the relocated City Hall by architects Augustus Laver and Thomas Fuller.

RESTAURANT
Soft Drinks, Cigars & Tobacco
OPEN FOR BUSINESS

Little remained of the City Hall wreckage after the earthquake and fire.

City Hall

City Hall *(right)* was completed in 1915, according to plans by Arthur Brown, Jr., and John Bakewell. With a dome slightly taller than the U.S. Capitol in Washington, D.C., this Beaux Arts–style gem anchoring a multistructure Civic Center was inspired by Paris's 17th-century Hôtel des Invalides. After sustaining damage in the 1989 Loma Prieta earthquake, the building underwent a seismic retrofitting and an expensive restoration that has brought it back to the grandeur it boasted in the days of Rolph.

A view of the domed rotunda inside City Hall

San Francisco Public Library

The city has had public libraries dating back to the 1870s, when cable-car promoter Andrew S. Hallidie advocated their development. However, the original Civic Center main branch at Larkin and McAllister streets *(left)*, designed by architect George Kelham, dates back to only 1917. The main library sustained damage during the 1989 Loma Prieta earthquake and was closed for several months. After a replacement library was built next door in the 1990s, Kelham's 1917 structure was redesigned to accommodate the city's Asian Art Museum, formerly based in Golden Gate Park. The new museum opened in the spring of 2003.

Kelham gave the library two high-ceilinged reading rooms in a library interior suggestive of an Italian palazzo.

The Asian Art Museum today rests in the former San Francisco Public Library building.

Right across Fulton Street from the old main library sits its equally grand and complementary substitute, designed by James Ingo Freed, who was responsible for the Holocaust Museum in Washington, D.C. This new library, with a central atrium and multistory reading rooms, opened in April 1996.

Opera House and Veterans Museum

Just behind City Hall on the west side of Van Ness Avenue sit two Beaux-Arts companion structures: Shown here in 1945 are the War Memorial Opera House on the left and the War Memorial Veterans Building on the right. Both opened in 1932 and were raised, in part, as monuments to World War I veterans. Since its opening, the Opera House has accommodated the San Francisco Opera and the San Francisco Ballet. Next door, the Veterans Building provides space for veterans organizations and contains the Performing Arts Library and Museum and the Herbst Theatre, where the charter establishing the United Nations was signed in 1945. From 1935 until 1995, when it moved to a new facility in the South of Market (SoMa) district, the San Francisco Museum of Modern Art occupied the upper floors of the Veterans Building.

Construction of the Opera House marked a cultural milestone for San Francisco, and residents enthusiastically took to it. Here, thousands line up in 1957 to buy tickets to *My Fair Lady*, which opened on July 8 for a six-week run.

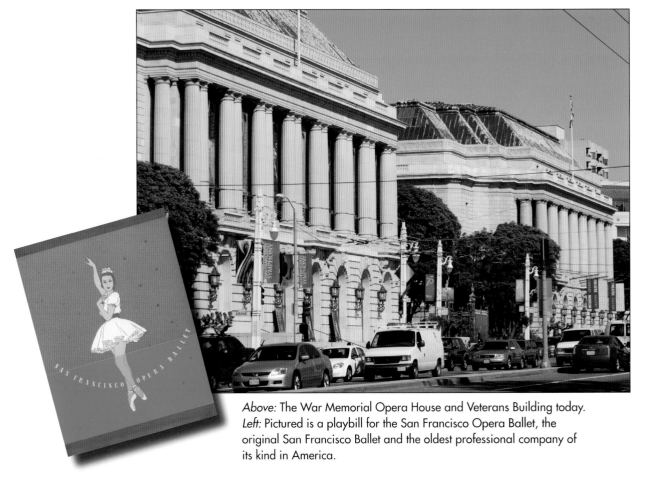

Above: The War Memorial Opera House and Veterans Building today. *Left:* Pictured is a playbill for the San Francisco Opera Ballet, the original San Francisco Ballet and the oldest professional company of its kind in America.

Crowds gathered at the Civic Center in September 1925 to celebrate the
Diamond Jubilee (75th anniversary) of California's admittance to the Union.

San Franciscans are known for their left-leaning politics,
and City Hall has long been a focal point of both protests and
celebrations. On November 6, 1968, Yippies—followers of
the Youth International Party, a theatrical and prankish political
movement that had grown out of the antiwar movement—gathered
on the lawn in front of City Hall to protest the ongoing Vietnam
War, the pending U.S. presidential contest (pitting two ex vice
presidents, Richard M. Nixon and Hubert H. Humphrey, against
each other), and politics in general.

Big Trouble in Little China

Reputedly the oldest and one of the largest Chinese enclaves outside of Asia, San Francisco's Chinatown is a reminder of the city's diverse heritage and is an exotic attraction in a place increasingly dependent on tourist dollars. It's tempting to think of it as a great stage, bountiful with Taoist temples, dim-sum parlors, and acupuncture clinics. Yet while there is much that is contrived about this quarter, Chinatown is also one of the nation's most densely populated residential districts.

The Chinese began arriving here in large numbers around the time of the gold rush, mostly from southern China's Guangdong province. They were hoping to escape the hardships of their homeland and fill their family coffers with the riches of *Gam Saan*— "Gold Mountain," as they called California. Greedy whites, however, didn't like Asians taking what they themselves wanted. So the Chinese either reworked claims supposedly tapped out already or found jobs on farms or in town as cooks, cigar makers, or domestic servants. Later, they and thousands more of their compatriots signed on with the Central Pacific Railroad to build the western part of the first transcontinental railway from Oakland, California, to Promontory, Utah. By the time all those Central Pacific laborers met their westbound counterparts from the Union Pacific at Promontory Summit on May 10, 1869, about 85 percent of the CP workforce was made up of Chinese "coolies," a racist term applied to low-status Asian and Indian immigrant workers.

SOCIAL STRUGGLES

Integrating the Chinese into San Francisco's population after the railway's completion caused political and social strains. Gathering on Stockton Street and around Portsmouth Square, the Chinese created a "Little China" inside larger San Francisco. Their segregation wasn't solely by choice, though; racial prejudice prevented them from finding housing outside of Chinatown. To maintain order within the community, merchants banded together to form the Chinese Six Companies, which acted as a philanthropic organization, a chamber of commerce, and oftentimes a peacekeeper as well. But in the 1870s, even that organization couldn't protect its people from angry white laborers who were resentful of competition in

Chinese workers put the finishing touches on the Southern Pacific Railroad's Secret Town trestle in the Sierra Nevada Mountains in 1877.

Left: Madame Chiang Kai-shek, wife of former Generalissimo of the national government of the Republic of China, tours Chinatown on March 25, 1943.

A man walks past an outdoor mural of a dragon in Chinatown, a symbol in Chinese mythology believed to ward off evil spirits.

a shrinking job market. Nor could it prevent politicians from instituting racist regulations, such as the 1876 "Pigtail Ordinance," which required that city-jail prisoners be shorn of any *queues,* waist-long pigtails worn proudly by the Chinese.

By 1882, when Congress suspended the immigration of Chinese labor into the United States and forbade the Chinese already here from bringing their families over, there were more than 20,000 Chinese living in San Francisco under crowded conditions. A large family of five or six people would sometimes live and run a small business in a single room. Bitter about their mistreatment and unhappy with the Six Companies for not doing more to help, gangs of hoodlums ("tongs") sprang up all over the quarter, punishing their brethren while expanding the availability of prostitution, drugs, and gambling—all attractive to the whites they most detested. Competing for control of those criminal enterprises, the tongs recruited "hatchet men," or hired killers, who prowled the neighborhood. Its underworld was very much above ground.

THE CHINESE ARE REBORN
When the 1906 earthquake and fire leveled Chinatown, not many Yankee San Franciscans voiced disappointment. Ironically, however, that disaster proved beneficial to the Chinese, for it destroyed City Hall and all of the birth records therein. Chinatown residents suddenly had as much proof of American citizenship as anybody else. ("Every

China Man was reborn out of the fire a citizen," remarked Maxine Hong Kingston in her 1980 book, *China Men.*) The neighborhood's ashes were barely cool before merchants began rebuilding, turning Chinatown into a tourist's notion of an Oriental fantasy. Breaking down the barriers of prejudice between Caucasian and Chinese San Francisco was a slower process. It was helped by the Great Depression, as relief was given without consideration for race, and World War II, when many Chinese Americans joined the armed forces. Repeal of the Chinese Exclusion Act in 1943, passage of the Immigration Act of 1965 (which abolished national-origin quotas), and the spread of middle-class Chinese to homes around the city further increased acceptance. By 1980, the population of Chinatown was 82,000.

Chinatown has seen declines over recent decades, as other Chinese communities have sprouted in the city's Sunset and Richmond districts and as Oakland's Chinatown has been revitalized. The neighborhood suffered economically after the Loma Prieta earthquake of 1989 led to the demolition of the Embarcadero Freeway, which had fed traffic into the area. It's said that overcrowded Chinatown isn't as popular a tourist attraction as it once was, falling behind both Fisherman's Wharf and Union Square. Yet this neighborhood doesn't exist for travelers alone. They may visit, spend money, and go home, but it's the people who came here to stay over the last 150 years who have made the more important investments.

Left: A busy street scene in Chinatown around the 1890s or early 1900s.
Above: Still a bustling epicenter of San Francisco, Chinatown today attracts locals and tourists alike.

PORTSMOUTH SQUARE

Portsmouth Square started out as an uneven, sloping block where potatoes were grown, Mexican *vaqueros* roped runaway cattle, and forty-niners swapped tales of fortunes sought and squandered. In 1854, the plaza was graded, fenced, and landscaped with gravel walks and abundant trees. The photograph above shows the site in 1866 looking west from Kearny Street.

When a nationwide influenza epidemic hit the city in October 1918, Judge John J. Sullivan vacated the close atmosphere of San Francisco's Hall of Justice directly across from Portsmouth Square in favor of the park. Sullivan is seated at the desk immediately in front of the Robert Louis Stevenson memorial.

In 1839, before Jasper O'Farrell shaped his downtown street pattern, a Swiss surveyor named Jean-Jacques Vioget created his own arrangement for what was then Yerba Buena. At the center, he placed a Spanish-style central plaza. The commons gained its current name after July 1846, when Captain John B. Montgomery disembarked from his vessel, the USS *Portsmouth*, and planted an American flag near the Mexican adobe house on the plaza, claiming California for the United States.

Until the 1870s, Portsmouth Square was the town's civic and entertainment hub. It originally sat a block west of Yerba Buena Cove, the beach running about where Montgomery Street does today. (That cove was later filled in, and the Financial District raised atop it.) Beside the plaza could be found the town's first hotel, its first public school, and one of its earliest city halls. Before that, the city hall building was occupied by showman Tom Maguire's former Jenny Lind Theater.

In 1873, people watched from the plaza as Andrew S. Hallidie's cable car made its maiden runs along Clay Street. Half a dozen years after that, a near penniless young Scottish writer named Robert Louis Stevenson lingered in Portsmouth Square, waiting for his lover to discard her philandering husband and join him. A monument in the plaza, created by sculptor Bruce Porter and architect Willis Polk, commemorates Stevenson's time there.

Although no longer considered the center of San Francisco, Portsmouth Square remains the "Heart of Chinatown." It has changed much over the decades, though. An underground garage was built under the park in the 1960s, and a $3.9 million renovation that began in the late 1980s added pagoda-shape structures.

Far left: A group of men hunker over a board playing checkers, as they've done for decades.
Left: Children watch as two boys play chess, circa 1935.

The terraced and bench-filled Portsmouth Square we know today—one of the few open-air retreats available in crowded Chinatown—is a generally peaceful spot, though concerns about its maintenance are periodically raised in the corridors of City Hall. Come good weather, the mornings find many people practicing tai chi. And all day long, old and young people alike people-watch in this place known as "Chinatown's living room."

In his 1933 book, *The Barbary Coast: An Informal History of the San Francisco Underworld,* American journalist-historian Herbert Asbury wrote that by 1855, Chinatown contained at least 26 opium dens. Here, a man smokes opium while holding his cat.

RACIAL TENSIONS

At first, it seemed as though the Chinese in San Francisco were looked upon as second- or third-class citizens, usurpers of the city's promise. Prejudice was overt, especially as the population of immigrants increased in the 1850s. In *The Annals of San Francisco,* a study of Bay Area life first published in 1855, writers Frank Soulé, John H. Gihon, and James Nisbet remarked that "the manners and habits of the Chinese are very repugnant to Americans in California. Of different language, blood, religion and character, inferior in most mental and bodily qualities, the Chinaman is looked upon by some as only a little superior to the negro, and by others as somewhat inferior." Animosities grew as Chinese businesses opened at the northern end of Sacramento Street. What had for so long been the center of town—around Portsmouth Square—took on a distinctly foreign appearance. It didn't help that Chinatown came to be associated with crime: gambling "hells," tong warfare and murder, and opium-smoking resorts. The neighborhood was portrayed as dirty and dangerous and a place that no God-fearing white person would enter. That is, except for those men and women in search of illicit pleasures, especially opium, a drug that had been used recreationally in China since the 15th century.

Chinatown was very much a bachelors' province during the first few decades of its existence, the men having come to the "Gold Mountain" in search of work. Of the few female inhabitants, many were brought to California as slave girls, smuggled through the Golden Gate disguised as boys and put to work as prostitutes. While some Chinese women were able to set themselves up as madams, most were peddled to pimps with operations along Morton Street (Maiden Lane) or on the Barbary Coast. In the middle and late 1870s, there were reportedly 1,500 to 2,000 Chinese prostitutes in San Francisco. The lives of these women were predictably hard and short. The photo here shows a Chinatown brothel in the 1890s, not long before most of the prostitution venues in San Francisco were swallowed by flames.

In 1870, San Francisco writer and editor Bret Harte published a narrative poem he called "Plain Language from Truthful James" in *The Overland Monthly*, but which has become better known as "The Heathen Chinee." Harte evidently intended his verse, which recounts the humorous tale of two miners conned at cards by a "naïve" Chinaman, as a satire of his era's white racist attitudes. However, it was interpreted by others as mocking the Chinese.

In 1900, the bubonic plague first surfaced in San Francisco, after a steamship docked in the city and dumped off both human passengers and rats infested with fleas carrying the so-called Black Death. Seven years later, the plague revisited the city, proving that Chinatown's complete destruction in 1906 had not wiped out all the harmful bacteria. Hoping to stop the disease's spread, an intensive rat hunt was launched, putting a bounty of ten cents on every rodent trapped and brought to one of the local health centers. (The photo above shows one roundup.) By the time the epidemic officially ended in 1909, San Francisco had counted about 286 cases of the bubonic plague and 199 deaths.

"THE CHINESE MUST GO!"

AFTER THE COMPLETION of the first transcontinental railroad in 1869, the Chinese who had been brought into California to help complete the Central Pacific's rail link to Promontory, Utah, were released to find other jobs—or *steal* other jobs at reduced wages, as many white workers in San Francisco saw it. Among those was Denis Kearney, an immigrant from County Cork, Ireland, who had owned a small drayage business before it went under in the wake of the financial Panic of 1873. He blamed the Chinese for souring the city's economy and set about provoking anti-Chinese ire among the working class.

Kearney knew what his audiences wanted to hear, and he delivered it as often as possible at the top of his lungs. The more outrageous he became and the more intolerance and hatred spilled from his tongue, the more respect Kearney gained among the laborers he sought to represent. Working himself into a scarlet-faced rage, he told the hordes of fellow bigots assembled to hear him speak in San Francisco's sandlots that "the Chinese must go!" It was a battle cry that made the foreign-born inhabitants of Chinatown hunch their shoulders for self-protection and incited whispers of anarchy among city residents.

Following a short stay behind bars after a demonstration on Nob Hill, Kearney went on to become politically influential, leading the socialist Workingman's Party of California. Kearney's demagoguery and its favorable reception even convinced Congress to pass the Chinese Exclusion Act of 1882, which suspended Chinese immigration into the United States for the next 60 years.

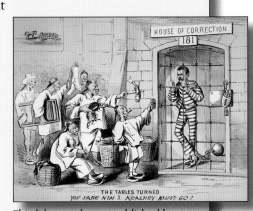

This lithograph was published by San Francisco book producer Isadore Nathan Choynski and appeared in 1877 or early 1878.

There's a theme-park air to modern Chinatown, with its templelike edifices, ornate lamps, heady scents of incense, and chirping crickets. This is one of the city's most popular tourist destinations and movie-making locales. Yet it's also a vital neighborhood, with English the foreign language on some streets.

SING CHONG BUILDING

We are so accustomed to seeing the red-tiled roofs, gracefully curving eaves, and dangling lanterns, which visually set Chinatown apart from the rest of San Francisco, that it's easy to forget this neighborhood hasn't always looked the way it does today.

For the first half century of its existence, the oldest quarter of town was Victorian in its architecture and looked pretty much like any other local area. However, after the fire and earthquake, Chinese merchants came up with an ingenious plan to counter a civic reconstruction committee's proposal that their neighborhood be moved to Hunter's Point, six miles away: They'd re-create Chinatown as an exotic-looking tourist attraction.

The architectural vernacular chosen to dominate the resurrected Chinatown was hardly authentic to Shanghai or Beijing. In fact, it was a whimsical interpretation by white architects of how they *thought* Chinese cities looked. Leading that makeover was Scottish-born designer T. Paterson Ross. Following the 1906 disaster, Ross and his engineer partner, Albert W. Burgren, captured a pair of commissions that did much to establish the architectural slang of today's Chinatown: the Sing Fat Building and the Sing Chong Building. (Both can be seen at left, the Sing Fat in the foreground and Sing Chong in the background.) They were raised together in 1908.

The same assortment of pagoda-inspired rooflines and shops filled with Far Eastern trinkets would be replicated in Chinatowns nationwide.

CHINATOWN STREET LIFE

Apparently, the streets of Chinatown have always been occupied with the business of commerce. Although some of the vocations have changed over the last century and a half, you still find a diverse streetscape here, abundant with fluttering Asian banners, ducks and dried sausages hanging in market windows, and crates brimming with odd fruits and vegetables. What's most remarkable may be the sheer breadth of goods for sale along these streets, from ornate porcelain vases to plastic, dragon-clawed backscratchers; from dried shark fins to brocade, satin qípáor dresses (Mandarin gowns) to the cheapest Buddha statues.

A mid-19th century Chinese market, spilling out onto a wooden sidewalk along Sacramento Street, offered a little bit of everything to customers who lived in the neighborhood's crowded tenements. It was on Sacramento in the 1850s that the district's first Chinese stores and organizations were established.

An 1890s vendor does a surprisingly brisk trade in plants and potted herbs.

This district's southern entrance at Grant Avenue and Bush Street is clearly identified by a flamboyantly decorated "dragon gate," designed by architect Clayton Lee and installed at that intersection in 1970. Slicing north from Market Street all the way to North Beach, Grant is said to be San Francisco's oldest road.

CHINATOWN ALLEYS

If Chinatown's crowded and colorful streets represent its face to the world, this neighborhood's alleyways have long symbolized its private life—and in the past, its not-so-hidden shame. A century ago, these narrow, shadowy passages, unevenly bedded with splintered boards, strung with laundry, and rampant with cooking odors, were fertile fields of wrongdoing frequented by whites and Asians alike. These alleys were also useful when thieves wanted to elude police and witnesses or when killers needed some concealed spot to commit their atrocities. During the late 1800s and early 1900s, as librarian Richard H. Dillon explained in his account of Chinatown's criminal heyday, *The Hatchet Men* (1962), "people all over California and the West, and eventually in all corners of the United States, came to know the names of the squalid Chinatown alleys which were the scenes of murders or pitched tong battles." These straits had names such as Stout's Alley, Cooper's Alley (also known as Ragpicker's Alley), and Waverly Place (near which Fun Jing Toy, a prosperous and deadly racketeer better known as "Little Pete," met his untimely end in 1897). There was no concealing the threats associated with some of these passages; St. Louis Alley, for instance, was casually known as Murderer's Alley.

An alleyway in Chinatown, circa 1907

Most of those lewd lanes are history now, wiped away by the disaster of 1906. Where prostitutes formerly worked their sordid trade and gamblers could be heard laying down bets on fan-tan games, it's far more common in the 21st century to see aged men with their grandchildren in tow, young women hustling home from their jobs, and stooped matrons toting plastic bags full of groceries for their families. Thanks to publicly funded restoration programs, a growing number of this district's 41 remaining alleys are being gussied up for tourists, who can be seen roaming their lengths in search of herb shops, hidden temples, the smartly painted balconies of Waverly Place, and the Golden Gate Fortune Cookie Factory in Ross Alley. Guided tours are even offered of several of the most prominent Chinatown passages.

A crowd of people gather outside Old St. Mary's Church for Good Friday services, April 7, 1944.

PLACES OF WORSHIP

The oldest Catholic church in San Francisco is the whitewashed La Misión de San Francisco de Asís (also known as Mission Dolores), dedicated in 1791 in what's now the Mission District. Six decades after the structure was built, a larger Gothic Revival competitor, Old St. Mary's Church (shown today at left), was added to the skyline. Designed by Englishman William Crain and Irishman Thomas England, it was constructed between 1851 and 1854 by Chinese laborers using granite and wood imported from China and brick and iron shipped west around Cape Horn. The finished church was dedicated on Christmas Eve 1854, and until 1891 it was the cathedral seat of the Catholic archdiocese of the Pacific Coast. Old St. Mary's has been decimated twice since by fires in 1906 and 1969, and it was damaged again in the 1989 Loma Prieta earthquake. Although this landmark predates Chinatown's existence, it's held firmly within its borders, standing in marked architectural contrast to the Sing Chong Building across Grant. In a not-so-subtle nod to its changing neighborhood, this place of worship boasts a Chinese Jesus, Joseph, and Mary in traditional Oriental attire.

Madame Chiang Kai-shek Visits

A crowd greeted Madame Chiang Kai-shek during her visit to Chinatown in the spring of 1943 at St. Mary's Square, a peaceful retreat located across California Street from Old St. Mary's Church. In this photograph, the wife of the president of the Republic of China (now Taiwan) can be seen standing with her entourage before a 12-foot-tall statue of Sun Yat-sen. That statue was commissioned in 1938 by Chinatown business leaders and was shaped of steel and stone by California-based Italian American sculptor Beniamino Bufano.

Tin How Temple

Thanks to ardent missionary efforts during San Francisco's first century, Chinatown still contains an unexpectedly large concentration of Christian churches. However, more traditional Chinese "joss houses" (where a diversity of Chinese saints, deities, and supernatural beings can be worshipped) are also found here. Among the most familiar is the Tin How (or Tien Hau) Temple on the top floor of 125 Waverly Place (right). Said to be the oldest Taoist temple in the United States, it dates back to the mid-19th century and is dedicated to Matsu (or Mazu), the Taoist goddess of sea and heaven. *Left:* A historical postcard celebrates the Tin How Temple's presence in Chinatown life. Then, like now, the temple was open to the public.

Right: San Francisco's Chinese New Year Parade is now said to be the largest celebration of its kind outside of Asia, and it remains one of the few lighted nighttime parades still scheduled in the United States. Here, a modern dragon winds through the streets of San Francisco.

Chinatown residents are never too young to carry on Chinese New Year traditions. Here, a boy holds a string of firecrackers that were integral to the 1936 festivities.

CHINATOWN ENTERTAINMENT

Although Chinatown has faced hardships over many decades, its residents have retained their capacity to enjoy themselves. In the 19th century, this quarter often erupted with spontaneous fireworks, and local celebrations of the Chinese New Year (otherwise known as the Lunar New Year, occurring in either January or February) date back to the gold rush days. Particularly prominent in parades and the New Year's celebrations are great flowing dragons being carried through the intersection of Dupont (Grant Avenue) and Washington streets in the 1880s *(center).* The dragon of Chinese mythology is a scaly, four-clawed, snakelike creature that symbolizes favorable power, rather than evil.

Police armed with guns and tear gas await gunmen who held up the Old Poodle Dog on July 14, 1957.

A menu from the Old Poodle Dog restaurant

Old Poodle Dog

Before 1900, Chinatown restaurants catered mainly to Chinese patrons. Guidebooks of the time often warned hungry Westerners away from Chinatown, saying that some of the cooking ingredients used might offend their palates. An eatery called Hang Far Low on Dupont between Clay and Sacramento streets did win some favorable recommendations beyond Chinatown in the late 1800s, but the district's most famous restaurant wasn't Chinese at all; it was French. The Poodle Dog, opened by a couple of Frenchmen in a shack at the corner of Dupont and Washington in 1849, was supposedly named for a small, white canine known as Ami, the pet of one of the owners' wives. By 1868, the establishment was drawing a remarkably large clientele with its European fare and flair (not to mention its reasonable prices—the Poodle Dog was said to offer the best dinner in town for less than a dollar). Later, it was able to move into a grander, multistory building on Chinatown's southern edge. Rebranded as the Old Poodle Dog, the restaurant served families and wealthy couples on its lower floors, reserving its upper ones for discreet engagements by the city's elite. Destroyed by fire in 1906, the Old Poodle Dog moved to the Union Square area. It survived in various incarnations and locations until the early 1980s.

Forbidden City

If you wanted a little song and dance with your evening meal—and maybe a strip show, too—the place to go was Charlie Low's Forbidden City. Though technically located just outside of Chinatown on Sutter near Stockton Street, the Forbidden City was a Chinese-themed nightclub and cabaret, taking its name from the Imperial Palace in Beijing. The club opened in 1938 and gained renown by treating mostly white audiences to all-Asian performances. Low played up the alien air of his acts, particularly the sensuality of his leggy Chinese women. He often nicknamed performers after white stars (the "Chinese Frank Sinatra," the "Chinese Fred and Ginger") to increase publicity. Acts ran the gamut from singers and musicians to magicians, dancers, and strippers. Celebrity guests such as film star Ronald Reagan and his first wife, Jane Wyman, and San Francisco politicians were photographed and featured in magazine spreads, increasing the club's national prominence. Low's Forbidden City even inspired Chinese American journalist C. Y. Lee to write his best-selling 1957 novel, *The Flower Drum Song*, which was later adapted as a musical. The club closed in 1962. *Right:* Two dancing stars pictured here in the 1930s or '40s.

A folder of souvenir photographs from the Forbidden City

CHINATOWN SCHOOLS

Attempts to establish a public school in San Francisco began in earnest in 1847, with Samuel Brannan's *California Star* newspaper drawing weekly attention to the absence of such an institution. By the following year, a tiny schoolhouse had been raised at Portsmouth Square, but its enrollment was restricted to white children only. In 1859, the Chinese School was founded in the basement of a chapel to accommodate the offspring of Asian immigrants. Because of low enrollment, however, it was soon converted into a night school. In 1871, following debate about whether minorities were legally due a free public education, San Francisco's superintendent shuttered the Chinese School. Another 14 years passed before a new Oriental Public School (named so Korean and Japanese students could also be assigned there) opened in Chinatown. The wooden academy, shown at right in 1914, was located on Clay Street between Powell and Joice.

A schoolroom scene, circa middle to late 1800s

After the 1906 disaster, Chinatown shed its bachelor-dominated roots and became a home for more families. Children proliferated. The Nam Kue Chinese School on Sacramento Street was erected in 1925 by the Fook Yum Benevolent Society as a place where children could learn about Chinese culture and language. Classes are held there at night and on weekends so that students today *(far right)* can attend regular school as well. *Above:* The obvious discomfort expressed in the faces of these early Chinese students is most likely due to their grueling schedule and generally strict teachers.

NORTH BEACH 1865.

A Place Apart

It's a fair question to ask: Where's the beach at North Beach? The answer: underground. This densely packed neighborhood with a small-town feel, located north of Chinatown and the Financial District, used to look quite different. Until the late 19th century, Yerba Buena Cove lapped at the feet of Telegraph Hill, and San Francisco Bay bit deep into the coastline. When the city created the Embarcadero, it filled and buried everything behind it, including the beach for which this district was named.

Over the decades, there have been many labels applied to North Beach, among them "Little Italy," in recognition of the numerous Italian immigrants who made this their home, and "San Francisco's Greenwich Village," recalling the bohemians and poets who once hung out here. But this neighborhood of coffeehouses, restaurants with checkered tablecloths, and view-seeking tourists isn't easily pigeonholed.

A WICKED PLACE

At its southern extreme, it elbows up against what was once the Barbary Coast. During the 19th and early 20th centuries, this quarter, which was centered on Pacific Avenue (or "Terrific Street," as residents called it), overflowed with bars and brothels and was an affront to everything clean-living San Franciscans wanted for their great city. An 1870 survey discovered that the Coast's underworld population

numbered 20,000—3,000 of whom made their living from prostitution.

The rest spent their days separating fools from their money in gambling joints, running ribald theaters, and managing an excess of drinking establishments. In 1875, the city of San Francisco issued some 2,000 liquor licenses, 304 of which went to places along the Barbary Coast. With such competition, watering holes had to be creative if they were to attract customers. One chained a live grizzly bear beside its entrance. Others, explained *Scribner's Monthly* magazine in 1875, "have organs that invite patrons to dally.... And some, in addition to a band, keep a female staff capable of waking thirst in a stone." Little remains of the Coast today, save for some historical edifices. A blues club called The Saloon, which opened in 1861 as Wagner's Beer Hall, and at least one adult bookstore, which might have

A view of Telegraph Hill from the Vallejo Street Wharf in the 1860s

Left: North Beach in 1865

Right: People now meet for a drink and more at sidewalk cafés along Columbus Avenue.

1928, when a city ordinance forbade their presence. It also used to be a well-rounded prominence. But captains and crews in search of ballast (a heavy substance such as gravel or stone to help keep their empty ships steady at sea) carved away at the eastern slope. Pieces of that hill are reportedly now part of cobblestone streets in China and South America. More rock and dirt were excavated in the 1860s and '70s to extend the land to the present-day San Francisco Bay seawall. Quarrying on Telegraph Hill continued until 1914.

Not long after U.S. military forces arrived on these shores in the 1840s, they installed a battery of cannons (the source of Battery Street's name) in the shadow of Telegraph Hill. However, those armaments were soon abandoned. During the gold rush, would-be prospectors raised tents and built rickety shacks on the hill slopes. In the 1850s, a raucous community known as Sydney Town sprang up along the hill's eastern base, its name referring to the Australian felons who had descended upon this frontier settlement in search of freedom and stayed to make a killing (often in more ways than one). Only slowly did Telegraph Hill attract more permanent and respectable residents. Today, it is prime real estate, punctuated at its crest by Coit Tower, one of San Francisco's premier vantage points and a beloved landmark.

seemed paltry fare to this area's original merrymakers, give little sense of the old quarter's bawdiness.

TELEGRAPH HILL
Rising from the east side of North Beach is Telegraph Hill. It used to be known as Goat Hill for the domesticated beasts that grazed over its slopes until

A PLACE TO RELAX
If North Beach has no beach, it at least has a village green of sorts: Washington Square, one of the most peaceful places in the city.

Coit Tower at the top of Telegraph Hill is a much-photographed symbol of the city.

COLUMBUS AVENUE

It is said that Columbus Avenue was once part of a dusty, rutted Spanish trail leading to the Presidio. None of those pioneers from Mexico could have anticipated the thoroughfare's frenzied future. *Inset:* In 1880, Columbus—then known as Montgomery Avenue—was a broad, plank-covered roadway. It carried wagons, horses, and hansom cabs through increasingly populated North Beach, without concern that rain would fill this roadway with impassable mud. *Bottom right:* By the 1940s, Montgomery had been rechristened Columbus Avenue, in part to avoid confusion with Montgomery Street, which passes north through the Financial District and marks the southeastern end of this thoroughfare. It's likely that the change was also made in recognition of the neighborhood's Italian heritage. *Top right:* Today, Columbus is one of San Francisco's busiest boulevards, trafficked by both North Beach residents and tourists alike and host to parades and occasional protest marches.

COLUMBUS TOWER

One of the more curious edifices on Columbus Avenue is Columbus Tower, formerly the Sentinel Tower (shown today in the foreground at left). Built in 1907 from plans by architects David Salfield and Herman Kohlberg, it was once the headquarters of corrupt Republican political boss Abe Ruef, who ascended to prominence on the back of Eugene Schmitz, president of the local Musicians' Union, whom attorney Ruef helped elect as mayor in 1901. With Schmitz in City Hall, Ruef became the real source of power in town, collecting bribes and protecting a series of prostitution businesses. A federal investigation of Schmitz and Ruef was eventually launched, and Schmitz was convicted of extortion and accepting bribes and sentenced to five years in San Quentin State Prison, while Ruef was subsequently convicted on multiple criminal counts and sentenced to 14 years in the same pen. *Above:* The Sentinel Building in the late 1920s. Columbus Tower once housed a recording studio used by the Kingston Trio and the Grateful Dead. It is currently owned by filmmaker Francis Ford Coppola and serves as the headquarters of his American Zoetrope studio.

Black Cat Café

For the local gay and lesbian community, the Black Cat Café *(above)* is something of a legend. It was opened in 1933 as a bohemian hangout, but its clientele changed after World War II, as gay servicemen discharged in San Francisco sought residency and understanding in this tolerant place. Its most memorable performer was José Sarria, a server who sang in full-flouncing drag and led bar patrons in rounds of "God Save Us Nelly Queens" (sung to the tune of "God Save the Queen"). In 1961, he ran for a seat on the Board of Supervisors, becoming the first openly gay political candidate in America. In the late 1940s, the Black Cat's straight owner, Sol Stoumen, protested police efforts to shutter his business by taking his case to the state Supreme Court—and he won the right to continue operating the Black Cat as an overtly gay bar. Nonetheless, harassment campaigns by city officials eventually convinced him to close the place in 1963. The space is now occupied by a tapas restaurant.

WALL OF SOUND

THE DIVERSITY OF NORTH BEACH—and of San Francisco, in general—is commemorated in the mammoth *Jazz Mural* painted on two sides of this building at the intersection of Columbus, Broadway, and Grant. Artist Bill Weber's work includes images of Italian fishermen, a Chinese Imperial Dragon, "Beat Generation" jazz musicians, eccentric 19th-century "Emperor" Joshua Norton, and former mayors Dianne Feinstein and Willie Brown. To the right in this photo is what was originally St. Francis of Assisi Church, established in 1849 as the first parish church in California. But, deprived of an active parish in the 1990s, it is now known as the National Shrine of St. Francis of Assisi.

Men gather outside nightclubs on Pacific Street in the Barbary Coast district in 1909.

BARBARY COAST

Growth of the Barbary Coast began right after the gold rush. Its name came into popular usage during the 1860s, probably the idea of some old sailor who saw similarities between this place and the more villainous Barbary Coast of North Africa. It would be a sinners' paradise for the next four decades, playing host to crime, prostitution, and the like. The Coast thumbed its nose at campaigns to curb its behavior. But what vigorous finger wagging and legislation couldn't accomplish, fire ultimately did. Little remained of this criminal carnival immediately after the 1906 disaster. Saloons and cathouses had to be rebuilt, yet the Coast never recovered its full measure of degeneracy. Instead, it

entered what popular historian Herbert Asbury called "an era of glamour and spectacularity, of hullabaloo and ballyhoo, of bright lights and feverish gayety, of synthetic sin and imitation iniquity." Shabby dives such as the Midway, the Hippodrome, and Spider Kelly's gave the air of a diabolical Disneyland, all bright lights and dim prospects. But the dark heart of the Barbary Coast eventually stopped beating. In 1913, the police force, which had for so long turned a blind eye to the misconduct practiced here, began cracking down on drinking and dancing. A year later, the Red Light Abatement Act gave the city the legal means to shutter this neighborhood's brothels.

Although decent San Franciscans publicly deplored the Barbary Coast, author Herbert Asbury contended that "secretly they were . . . enormously proud of their city's reputation as the Paris of America and the wickedest town on the continent." Visitors to the city rarely passed up a tour of this quarter. But after 1910, dance halls and saloons like the Moulin Rouge (shown below in 1911) drew as many people to the neighborhood as did prostitution and lewd variety programs. In 1913, the Moulin Rouge was closed temporarily for contributing to the delinquency of minors, an order highlighting how many of the district's employees were girls barely in their teens.

At its height, Barbary Coast prostitution was transacted on different basic levels. At the bottom, women rented narrow stalls marked off by curtains. One rung up were the dance halls, which offered amateur entertainment and "pretty waiter girls" who served men whatever their libidos craved. At the trade's upper end, parlor houses run by madams, who sought a modicum of stature in their community, operated out of former private residences that sported antique furnishings and maids. In 1917, police began forcibly eliminating houses of prostitution. In response, hundreds of "underworld women" protested their maltreatment—sometimes in churches (above), much to the consternation of Sunday worshippers.

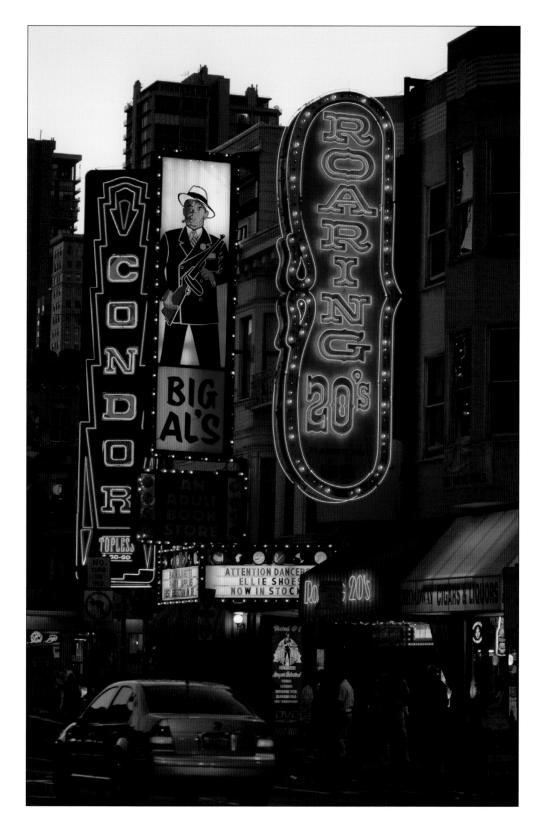

Hoping to bury what remained of the Barbary Coast, the city redesignated that quarter the "International Settlement" and in the 1930s raised a huge archway with the new moniker over Pacific Avenue. Clubs such as the Barbary Coast, though (where Frank Sinatra got a job in the 1957 film *Pal Joey*), were neon reminders of the area's indecent past. As late as 1964, when Carol Doda kicked off the American topless-dancing craze at the Condor Night Club at Broadway and Columbus, the Coast still had the ability to shock. But decades later, its bars and adults-only emporia are pale reminders of what was. Even a notorious, larger-than-life rendering of Ms. Doda, once featured on the Condor, was taken down in the early 1990s. Today, the Condor still displays its historic sign, but it operates as a sports bar, and the infamous Barbary Coast is part of the Jackson Square Historical District, best known for its restored, pre-1906 buildings and interior-decor shops.

CITY LIGHTS BOOKSTORE

City Lights, at Columbus Avenue and Broadway, is the town's best-recognized independent bookstore. Named after a 1931 Charlie Chaplin silent film and founded in 1953 by poet Lawrence Ferlinghetti and Peter D. Martin, an instructor at San Francisco State College, City Lights took over space in a triangular 1907 building that had previously been occupied by Italian bookseller A. Cavalli & Company *(top)*. (A. Cavalli & Company opened in 1880 and is still operating as Cavalli Italian Bookstore at 1441 Stockton Street.) The City Lights business plan was to sell paperback books only—enough to pay the rent on a second-floor office space occupied by an early and short-lived pop-culture magazine, also called *City Lights*. Two years after it opened, the shop began its own publishing imprint. It triggered much controversy by adding to its list "Beat Generation" author Allen Ginsberg's *Howl and Other Poems* (1956), which forthrightly depicted illicit drug use and homosexuality, and Ginsburg became the target of a landmark obscenity trial. (The title poem was eventually judged to have "redeeming social importance.")

During the half century since, City Lights has expanded both in size and stock. The bookstore now retails hardcover releases as well as paperbacks but still maintains its antiauthority attitudes, especially regarding political books and poetry. In 2001, the San Francisco Board of Supervisors declared City Lights an official historic landmark *(bottom)*, citing its contributions to America's literary development and its championing of First Amendment protections.

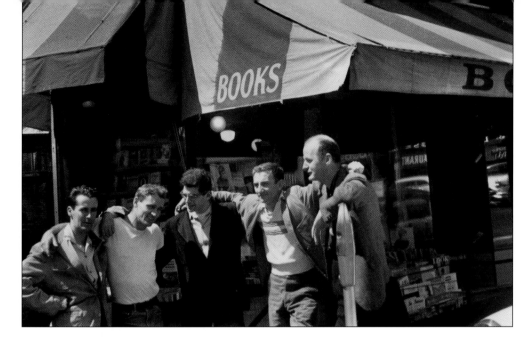

America's "Beat" Writers

It didn't take long for City Lights to become known as the spiritual home of America's "Beat" writers, people such as Ginsberg, Jack Kerouac, Gregory Corso, William S. Burroughs, and Gary Snyder, who shocked Eisenhower-era America with their language and literary themes. Many members of that movement frequented this bookshop, reading and rapping. The Beat writers were considered "something akin to American literature's first rock stars," as Steven Watson wrote in *The Birth of the Beat Generation* (1995). *Above:* The five Beat authors gathered outside City Lights in 1956 are, from left to right, Bob Donlin, a poet from Massachusetts who was featured in two of Jack Kerouac's novels under the moniker Bob Donnelly; Neal Cassady, who's mentioned in *Howl* as the "secret hero of these poems" and appeared as Dean Moriarty in Kerouac's *On the Road;* Allen Ginsburg; artist Robert LaVigne; and bookshop proprietor Ferlinghetti.

Authentic Beats were pretty thin on the ground in late-1950s North Beach. But the national publicity surrounding their intellectual movement brought forth a wave of "beatniks," a term coined by *San Francisco Chronicle* columnist Herb Caen in 1958, referring to young male and female hipsters who strove to imitate the free-spirited lifestyle of the characters in books by Kerouac and his ilk. Caen characterized them as "far out of the mainstream of society." However, they became fixtures in venues such as the Vesuvio Café. Founded in 1948 by Henri Lenoir (shown above with a tongue-in-cheek window display), this small, bohemian-style saloon holds forth on Columbus, immediately south of City Lights. Vesuvio is a late-night hangout and only closes between 2 and 6 A.M. It's filled with Beat memorabilia and boasts a much-photographed mural in the alley, in which the bar's name is spelled out in wine labels *(left).*

NORTH BEACH LIFE

When it designated North Beach as one of the top ten great neighborhoods in 2007, the American Planning Association (APA) applauded this historic district's "eclectic mix of mom-and-pop shops, nightclubs, and polyglot character." The APA, which represents urban and regional planners nationwide, added that "North Beach is, in many ways, a traditional neighborhood. It's rarely more than a few blocks walk to find a grocer, bakery, barbershop, hardware store, church, school, or park. What cannot be found in the neighborhood are chain stores and fast-food outlets. And that's by design."

Although there's been considerable change in the population of North Beach (it's now approximately 50 percent Asian), the Italian character of this place is still evident in its ubiquity of delis, unpretentious restaurants, and sidewalk cafés—all places that promote interaction between residents. The women seen shopping for meat, fruit, and vegetables in North Beach in 1943 *(above)* might feel equally at home at Molinari's Delicatessen on modern Columbus Avenue today *(right)*.

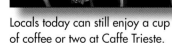

Locals today can still enjoy a cup of coffee or two at Caffe Trieste.

North Beach Coffeehouses

Although Seattle is currently considered the coffee capital of the United States, North Beach residents were wired on caffeine long before those rain-washed Washingtonians ever thought coffee was hot. Given that Italy's taste for the roasted bean dates back to at least 1645, when the first coffee shop was opened in that country, it's no surprise that immigrants from there brought their brews to this neighborhood. Today, there are numerous Italian coffeehouses crowded within the borders of North Beach, perhaps the most widely known being Caffe Trieste at Vallejo Street and Grant Avenue. Opened in 1956 by Italian immigrant Giovanni Giotta, this has long been a gathering place for bohemians and struggling artists. Beat writers Jack Kerouac and Allen Ginsberg were once regulars here, and Francis Ford Coppola spent months occupying a table along the back wall, wrestling into shape the screenplay for his 1972 epic The Godfather. In his work titled "Café Trieste: San Francisco," former U.S. poet laureate Joseph Brodsky wrote of this place: "Nothing has changed here. Neither the furniture nor the weather." Patrons prefer it that way.

Old Spaghetti Factory

Italians moving into the North Beach area in the late 19th century naturally brought with them their traditional cuisine—pastas, sauces, and their fondness for fish. It didn't take long for San Francisco's non-Italian population to become interested in what was being served on the tables of this growing Little Italy. Restaurants such as Coppa's in the old Montgomery Block, Vanessi's on Broadway, and Fior d'Italia (which opened in North Beach in 1886 and continues to satisfy appetites in the San Remo Hotel on Mason Street), set the pace for others to follow. One of the others was Frederick Kuh's Old Spaghetti Factory (above), which Kuh opened in 1956 in a defunct old pasta factory on Green Street. Kuh filled his barnlike building with a generous assortment of Victoriana and bordello furnishings—and San Franciscans loved it. Visitors did, too. Former Illinois Governor Adlai Stevenson is said to have made Kuh's place his unofficial local campaign headquarters during his second presidential campaign in 1956. But in the early 1980s, Kuh finally sold the restaurant and moved to Europe. Another Italian dining spot now fills the Spaghetti Factory space.

TELEGRAPH HILL

At 284 feet, Telegraph Hill was an excellent vantage point from which to observe ships passing through the Golden Gate. In 1850, a wooden tower was erected atop the hill to keep the people below apprised of maritime activity, and this crude "telegraph" system evidently gave the point its moniker. Three years later, an electric telegraph was installed at Point Lobos, near the Golden Gate, making the windmill-like semaphore station obsolete.

In 1876, a group of businessmen (including George Hearst, the father of newspaper mogul William Randolph Hearst) purchased and donated to the city almost two acres at the top of Telegraph Hill. They insisted that the site be preserved as Pioneer Park. However, the city had committed its meager park development funds to constructing Golden Gate Park, so little could be done in the way of improvements. Hoping to foster interest in the hilltop, local real-estate speculator Frederick Layman proposed building a resort beside the park property and running a cable-car line to it. Although the city nixed his cable railway, he did build a three-block funicular system up Greenwich Street in 1884. And at the top of Telegraph Hill, he opened his Pioneer Park Observatory. A "time ball" atop a mast on the main pavilion dropped at noon every day, helping ships' captains to keep their chronometers accurate. (That time ball and a funicular car can both be seen in the photo above.) Unfortunately, the landmark castle gained a reputation for hosting hoodlums, the funicular was discontinued after a decline in ridership and a well-publicized wreck, and the resort sat abandoned for several years before burning to the ground in 1903.

The fortresslike observatory at the crest of Telegraph Hill may be history, but this mount isn't entirely bereft of turrets and battlements. There's still Julius' Castle, an eccentrically designed restaurant on the hill's eastern slope. Made of redwood and maple recovered from San Francisco's 1915 Panama-Pacific International Exposition, it was opened in 1922 by Italian immigrant Julius Roz. It served as a speakeasy for the upper crust during Prohibition and has since become popular with diners craving panoramic views of the Bay.

COIT TOWER

Eliza Wychie "Lillie" Hitchcock developed a passion for fire-fighting early, and she never lost it. The New York–born daughter of an army physician, she was brought to San Francisco in 1851. According to legend, a member of Knickerbocker Engine Company No. 5, a local contingent of volunteer firefighters, rescued her as a girl from a burning building. Enchanted by this act of heroism, she took to cheering on and running after her beloved Knickerbockers whenever she saw them charging toward a climbing fire. Her devotion to the men of Engine Company No. 5 was so strong that in 1863, the Knickerbockers made her an honorary volunteer firefighter.

In 1868, "Firebelle Lillie" wed Benjamin Howard Coit, the well-respected "caller" at this city's leading mining exchange. When Lillie died in 1929 at age 86, she left behind $50,000 for a monument to the city's gallant firefighters (later raised in Washington Square) and another $100,000 for city beautification. With the latter funds, the city hired Henry T. Howard, an architect in the office of Arthur Brown, Jr., who had designed City Hall, to fashion a fitting memorial to Lillie Hitchcock Coit atop Telegraph Hill. What Howard came up with was a fluted, 210-foot-tall, art-deco tower that was completed in 1933. Suggestions that it is supposed to resemble a fire-hose nozzle don't hold water. A 12-foot-tall bronze statue of Italian explorer Christopher Columbus, sculpted by Vittorio di Colbertaldo and dedicated in 1957, stands in front of Coit Tower, looking west toward the Pacific Ocean.

For many, the view from the top of Coit Tower is the draw. Others come for the lobby full of murals *(left)*. President Franklin Roosevelt's Works Progress Administration paid 26 artists to create huge paintings portraying California life during the Great Depression. The images of the railroad industry, farming, and more were originally criticized for being subversive and left wing, and it delayed Coit Tower's opening for several weeks.

The Other Side of Telegraph Hill

Prior to the gold rush, the east side of Telegraph Hill was smoothly graded and extended almost all the way to the Bay. But quarrying and erosion conspired to make the slope steeper. A growing San Francisco population insisted on building homes all over the hill, but roads couldn't be laid up the steep east side grades. The best and cheapest solution was to construct wooden staircases. *Right:* In the 1880s, the steps straddling Telegraph Hill from the waterfront to the Pioneer Park Observatory served an increasing number of working-class residents.

Left: Today's Filbert Steps continue to provide essential access for residents living on this face of the North Beach mount. Offering views of the Bay for both tourists and locals, the stairs rise in three sections from Sansome Street to Coit Tower. There are almost 400 steps in all. Lush gardens line these flights, as do some private dwellings that date back to the 1870s and '80s. (Telegraph Hill cottages survived the 1906 fire, it's said, because residents banded together with buckets of water and barrels of wine that had been fermenting in the basements of Italian families and dumped it all onto the threatening flames below.)

Wild Parrots of Telegraph Hill

This knoll's abundant cherry-headed and blue-crowned parakeets may be the descendents of former house pets, exotic wild birds brought to the United States from the dry forests of Peru and Ecuador before their importation was banned in the 1990s. Estimates are that 130 to 200 of these colorful, squawking tree-dwellers now inhabit the Telegraph Hill slopes. Many of them were given names by Mark Bittner, who wrote a 2004 memoir, *The Wild Parrots of Telegraph Hill*. Bittner, a once homeless and unemployed musician, became the birds' caretaker. In 2007, San Francisco made it a misdemeanor (punishable with a $100 fine) to feed these feathered creatures in city parks, a ban endorsed by Bittner and ornithologists who contend that feeding them brings the birds closer to the ground and makes them targets for predators.

For decades, Telegraph Hill existed as a fairly isolated neighborhood inhabited by artists and blue-collar immigrants. That all changed after World War II, though, as more affluent families began moving into the Victorian and early 20th century homes crowded onto this peak. The Hill, as residents call it, is one of this city's most desirable neighborhoods today, despite the difficulty of ever finding free parking on its inclines.

WASHINGTON SQUARE

When city surveyor William Eddy submitted a vastly expanded plan for the town, just a few years after Jasper O'Farrell platted San Francisco in 1847, it included four green spaces: Portsmouth Square, Union Square, a never-constructed park near Folsom and 7th streets (in today's South of Market area), and Washington Square on Union Street between Powell and Stockton. The last commons was carved out of what had been a sprawling ranch owned by Juana Briones de Miranda, a Mexican American entrepreneur who pioneered Yerba Buena in the 1830s and '40s. In the 1860s, chain gangs were brought in to clear and landscape the space, and the resulting plaza became popular with promenading couples. In the 1870s, Montgomery Avenue (renamed Columbus Avenue in 1909) was sliced across the park's southwest corner, leaving behind a triangular, poplar-shaded pocket park that is technically still part of the original.

North Beach residents and politicians clashed over a proposal to excavate Washington Square and tuck a parking garage beneath it in the late 1950s. After that plan bit the dust, celebrated American landscape architect Lawrence Halprin (who would go on to create the Civic Center's United Nations Plaza and Ghirardelli Square) was brought in to redesign the park. He and landscaper Douglas Baylis, a North Beach dweller, developed an arrangement of paths and plantings that makes the setting more inviting than its previous presentation. Tai chi practitioners gather in the square during morning hours, amateur art shows are periodically held in this spot, and the Telegraph Hill parrots often come down for a visit.

Volunteer Firemen Memorial

Above: In addition to the money Lillie Hitchcock Coit left behind in her will for city beautification, which went toward constructing Coit Tower, she specified that another $50,000 be spent on a monument to her beloved firefighters. To honor that wish, Armenian American San Francisco sculptor Haig Patigian was hired to fashion the great bronze Volunteer Firemen Memorial that stands in the southwest corner of Washington Square. The sculpture features a 14-foot-high trio of firefighters, one of whom carries a woman in his arms while another holds a fire hose. This statue was dedicated in a ceremony attended by many of the city's firefighters on December 3, 1933. During the gold rush years, San Francisco was devastated half a dozen times by great infernos. Until 1866, the firefighters were volunteers, men prepared to dive into flaming buildings to save occupants. Their heroism was heralded with an inscription on the front of this monument's nine-foot concrete base:

TO COMMEMORATE THE

VOLUNTEER FIRE DEPARTMENT

SAN FRANCISCO

1849–1866

Benjamin Franklin Monument

According to *Chronicle* writer Carl Nolte, the late, great San Francisco newspaper columnist Herb Caen reveled in reciting the "contradictory virtues" of Washington Square: "It is a square that isn't a square, the heart of North Beach, which isn't a beach. Washington Square isn't on Washington Street and has a statue of Benjamin Franklin instead of George Washington. The statue was erected by H. D. Cogswell, a teetotaler, but the square is surrounded on three sides by bars and restaurants and on the fourth by a church."

The Franklin monument *(above)* was given to the city in 1879 by Henry D. Cogswell, a Connecticut-born dentist and advocate against alcohol, who came to San Francisco during the gold rush and spent his later life trying to erect public water fountains across the United States.

Washington Square's Franklin statue was moved to its present location in 1904. It, too, had been designed as a drinking fountain. Reports, however, say it never functioned well in that capacity.

Washington Square has long been a gathering place, one of the few large open spaces in tightly packed North Beach. *Above:* Fashionable older Italian gents enjoy the sun and some conversation at this park in the fall of 1956. *Right:* The family of Swiss-born photographer J. B. Monaco, whose studies of this neighborhood in the late 19th and early 20th centuries earned him acclaim as the "dean of North Beach photographers," rests on a bench in the plaza, circa 1904.

SAINTS PETER AND PAUL CHURCH

The most prominent landmark on Washington Square is the brilliant white, Gothic-influenced Saints Peter and Paul Church. But that wasn't always so. In fact, this Roman Catholic parish's original and more rustic home was located one block to the east at the corner of Grant and Filbert streets. The church was founded in 1884, but the 1906 quake and fire reduced it to rubble. Today's church opened in 1924 and was designed in a complementary blend of Gothic and Romanesque styles by Charles Fantoni. It is particularly notable for its twin spires soaring 191 feet into the sky and its rather ironic address: 666 Filbert Street.

This place of worship may be best remembered for its role in the life of baseball legend Joe DiMaggio, who had grown up in this city and played for the minor-league San Francisco Seals before signing with the New York Yankees. The slugger was baptized, took his first communion, and was confirmed in this church. Then in November 1939, DiMaggio married actress Dorothy Arnold here. They later divorced. In 1954, he wanted to wed Marilyn Monroe in the same place, but he was forbidden from exchanging "I do's" since he hadn't yet won an annulment from his previous union with Arnold. Instead, the "Yankee Clipper" eloped with Monroe to San Francisco City Hall, and after their civil ceremony, they came here to have their pictures taken on the cathedral's steps. Monroe filed for divorce only nine months later. The last link between DiMaggio and this church dates back to 1999, when the funeral for the late, great center fielder was held here.

The original and less grandiose Saints Peter and Paul Church can be seen in the background to the left in the mid to late 1800s.

Original plans apparently called for this house of worship to be covered with mosaics, but the plans were set aside. Still, there is a mosaic inscription of the opening words from Dante's *Paradiso* spanning the facade, which translated is "The glory of Him who moves all things penetrates and glows throughout the universe." A piece of that inscription can be seen above the building's main entrance.

The stunning Saints Peter and Paul Church today

Above It All

San Francisco has its ups and downs. Literally. You go up one hill and down the next. In its youth, San Francisco had only seven hills, and they emulated the seven hills of Rome. There was Telegraph Hill, Nob Hill, Russian Hill, Rincon Hill, Mount Sutro, Twin Peaks, and Mount Davidson. Today, however, this town boasts 43 official hills (plus ten or more unofficial peaks, making San Francisco the second hilliest city in the world after La Paz, Bolivia).

Originally called California Street Hill after the historic thoroughfare that runs east to west over its summit, Nob Hill's present moniker may derive from "nabob," a corruption of the east Indian word "nawab," which applied to Muslim nobles. More likely, it is a variation on "knob," meaning knoll or rounded hill. Residences and other structures began crawling up this hill after the gold rush, but its steep slopes were a discouragement to transit until the 1870s, when a cable-car line was run up California Street. By then, Nob Hill had become *the* place to live. Its heights were filled with ostentatious mansions built by the "Big Four" railroad barons (responsible for laying the western portion of North America's first transcontinental railway) and the "Silver Kings" of Nevada's Comstock Lode. Some Nob Hill residents had formerly been nestled in homes in Rincon Hill or South Park, but they were forced out by economic and commercial changes in those neighborhoods. Nob Hill proved an ideal perch on which to display their new affluence, if not also their refinements. *The Argonaut,* a highly respected literary journal of the late 19th century, took hill residents to task for their exhibitions of greed by remarking, "When a San Franciscan gets to be immensely wealthy, he builds a palace of a stable with marble halls, Brussels carpets, and hot and cold water in every stall; a Chicago millionaire builds a college."

A NEW NOB HILL

Nob Hill's elite preeminence ended, though, when the 1906 earthquake and fire destroyed old San Francisco. Almost nothing atop that knoll survived the flames save for the fancy facades of silver mogul James Flood's brownstone and the Fairmont Hotel, both of which were gutted but not completely destroyed. After the catastrophe, local executives relocated to Pacific Heights or moved out of the city completely, preferring the less crowded environs down the Peninsula. Nob Hill instead sprouted multiple luxury dwellings,

Young boys walk hand-in-hand down the steps of Pacific Heights Hill in 1955.

Left: Motorcyclists cruise up winding Lombard Street in the 1920s.

A cable car takes passengers down California Street in 1882.

belted out what would become his signature song, "I Left My Heart in San Francisco."

The spreading fingers of cable-car tracks around San Francisco in the late 1800s brought with them a greater reach of population. (The growth of cable cars is well documented in Nob Hill's Cable Car Museum at the corner of Washington and Mason streets.) Pacific Heights, to the west of Nob Hill, featured little more than a few one-story cottages until 1877, when Andrew Hallidie's Clay Street cable line was extended to Van Ness Avenue. After that, the area began filling up with individual Victorian residences and wooden row houses, including the "painted ladies" that for many people are symbolic of San Francisco. But the nouveau riche also constructed such opulent homes as the Bourn Mansion on Webster Street and the Whittier Mansion, a Romanesque structure on Jackson Street and Laguna

among them architect James Francis Dunn's 1921 Parisian-style Chambord Apartments at Sacramento and Jones streets. And it grew thick with exclusive hotels such as the Mark Hopkins and Stanford Court, both raised where their millionaire namesakes had once owned homes, and the Fairmont, which was one of the city's most famous accommodations. It was at the Fairmont in 1962 that vocalist Tony Bennett first

that was erected in 1896 for a paint and glass company executive. The mansion is supposedly haunted. Although many of Pacific Heights' dwellings were spared in the 1906 disaster, one of the most grandiose, German-born Claus Spreckels's enviable stone château at the corner of Van Ness and Clay was gutted beyond repair. Spreckels reportedly offered firefighters $1 million to save his mansion, but the place was already too far gone.

RUSSIAN HILL
Like Pacific Heights, Russian Hill enjoys exceptional views of Alcatraz, Fisherman's Wharf, and the Golden Gate. Preserving those fine sights has provoked skirmishes in the past over building-height restrictions and landmark preservation. This prominence derives its name from the gold rush–era discovery of a small Russian cemetery near its summit, the graves probably belonging to men from Fort Ross, an early 19th century Russian outpost north of San Francisco. In 1852, the town's first legal execution took place on Russian Hill's western slope, when Spaniard José Forner was hanged for killing a man he said had pilfered his gold dust. The hill's history hasn't always been so colorful, though it was here in the 1950s in a tiny house at 29 Russell Street that author Jack Kerouac dwelt, with fellow Beat Generation icon Neal Cassady, while he penned *On the Road.* And Macondray Lane, a small, wooded pedestrian path on the mount's southeast side, was the inspiration for "Barbary Lane" in Armistead Maupin's *Tales of the City.*

Modern streetcars glide past the mansion once owned by Comstock Lode "Silver King" James C. Flood.

NOB HILL

The wealthy families who raised their wooden castles on Nob Hill's summit in the late 19th century spared no expense in trying to outbuild and outdecorate each other. A classic example was the residence of Mark Hopkins at California and Mason streets (shown at right, circa late 1800s). The treasurer and most senior member of the "Big Four" owners of the Central Pacific Railroad, Hopkins delegated the construction of this high Victorian Gothic home to his wife, Mary, a devotee of romantic fiction. She, in turn, kept local architects John Wright and George Sanders and the hired builders busy adding turrets, gingerbread embellishments, chimneys, and sculpted lions. This went on until even her husband worried that his money was going to create the city's foremost eyesore. Hopkins might have considered himself lucky to die in 1878, before his mansion was finished. Following Mary's death in 1891, it became home to the San Francisco Art Association, before being destroyed in the 1906 disaster.

From left to right stand the Crocker, Colton/Huntington, and Flood mansions, circa 1905.

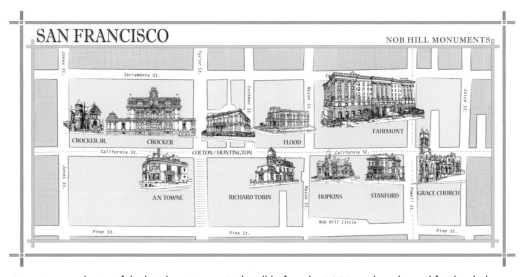

An artistic rendering of the lavish estates on Nob Hill before the 1906 earthquake and fire leveled most of them. The only structures still standing today are the Flood mansion and the Fairmont Hotel.

While his Nob Hill neighbors erected their palaces made mostly of wood, Comstock Lode "Silver King" James C. Flood built his of Connecticut brownstone—a foresighted decision, because it was the only one to survive the fire of 1906. Designed by Augustus Laver (who had been the original architect for the first City Hall at Civic Center), the mansion is located on the northwest corner of California and Mason streets, and wings were added in the early 20th century by architect Willis Polk. It's now home to the exclusive, Republicans-and-men-only Pacific Union Club.

The mansion of railroad mogul and former California Governor Leland Stanford at Powell and California streets was also a showpiece. Designed by S. C. Bugbee & Son and decorated by New York designers Auguste Pottier and William P. Stymus, the house was completed in 1876. It featured a private art gallery, from the center of which rose tall plants that were filled with mechanical birds set to sing at the push of a button.

Next door to the Flood mansion, on what's now the site of Huntington Park, stood the white, two-story neoclassical residence of "General" David D. Colton, business manager for the Big Four. (The home is shown on the right in this photo, circa late 1800s.) After Colton died in 1878, Collis P. Huntington, another of the Central Pacific executives, seized his palazzo from the widow in a sting that incited a sensational trial, exposing the railway's political manipulations. Like Stanford's dwelling, Colton's was designed in the early 1870s by S. C. Bugbee & Son. The home of Charles Crocker, the last of the Big Four to build atop Nob Hill, can be seen west of that mansion at California and Taylor. In 1877, he commissioned Arthur Brown, chief civil engineer of the Central Pacific (and the father of future City Hall designer Arthur Brown, Jr.) to create a mammoth Second Empire–style château.

Grace Cathedral

One of the most imposing edifices on present-day Nob Hill is Grace Cathedral, located on land previously occupied by the mansions of Charles Crocker and his banker son, William. After their homes were leveled by the 1906 blaze, this site was donated to the Episcopal Church for a new cathedral. It would replace the brick Grace Church (consecrated in 1862), at the corner of California and Stockton streets, which had also been destroyed. The Reverend James Smith Bush, great-great-grandfather of President George W. Bush, had served as rector of Grace Church in the late 1860s. Today's concrete Grace Cathedral was conceived by Lewis P. Hobart, who also created Golden Gate Park's Steinhart Aquarium and the Bohemian Club on Taylor Street. The cathedral was designed in a French Gothic style reminiscent of Paris's Notre Dame Cathedral. Construction began in 1910 but wasn't finished until 1964 when a pair of bronze gilded doors—replicas of 15th-century gates created for the Florence Bapistry in Florence, Italy, by sculptor Lorenzo Ghiberti—were installed at the cathedral's main entrance (inset).

Fairmont and Mark Hopkins Hotels

With fellow "Silver Kings" James C. Flood, William S. O'Brien, and John W. Mackay, Irishman James G. Fair made a fortune from Nevada's Comstock Lode, beginning in 1859. Fair went on to invest in other enterprises, and in 1881 was appointed to the U.S. Senate from Nevada. Before he died in 1894, he intended to build the West's costliest mansion on Nob Hill property, directly across Mason Street from Flood's immense home. Instead, his ambitious daughters, Theresa and Viginia, set about constructing a luxurious hotel on that site in 1902, the Fairmont (top, circa today). They hired Canadian-born, former Illinois architects Merritt and James Reid as designers. In early April 1906, with the hotel mostly finished and awaiting furniture, the Fair daughters sold it in exchange for two office buildings downtown. No sooner had the deal closed than the earthquake and fire devastated San Francisco, and the Fairmont was gutted. To restore their blaze-blackened building, the new owners engaged local designer Julia Morgan. She was the first woman to graduate with an architecture degree from Paris's prestigious École des Beaux-Arts and later became famous for designing William Randolph Hearst's palatial estate near San Simeon, California. Only a year later, the seven-story Fairmont opened to tremendous fanfare—and the relief of its owners.

In 1926, the 19-story Mark Hopkins Hotel (bottom, in the 1950s), owned by mining engineer George D. Smith and designed by San Francisco architects Peter Weeks and William P. Day, opened on the site once occupied by the flamboyant mansion of railroad tycoon Mark Hopkins. Both hotels are now historic landmarks.

Above: Servers await the arrival of their guests in the dining room of the Fairmont in 1907. Its dining rooms were some of the most ostentatious in town.

Andrew Hallidie sits in the front row *(middle)* on one of the first cable-car voyages along Clay Street.

CABLE CARS

In the late 1860s, horse-drawn streetcars were this city's principal means of public conveyance. However, Andrew Smith Hallidie was about to revolutionize local transportation. Born in England in 1836, Hallidie arrived in California in 1852 with his father, a Scottish engineer who'd spent years developing and patenting techniques for the production of wire ropes. The enthusiasm for invention was passed down to young Andrew, who by the time he turned 19 had already built a suspension bridge stretching more than 200 feet across the middle fork of the gold-bearing American River. This was his initial large-scale application of the cable technology that had consumed his father. But it would not be the last. On August 1, 1873, Hallidie employed a refined version of that same technology to launch San Francisco's first cable car from the top of Nob Hill down Clay Street toward Portsmouth Square.

Many people had scoffed at this young engineer's venture. They dubbed it "Hallidie's Folly." Yet the cable-car concept seems almost elementary now. It required the installation of an endless loop of steel rope moving continuously in a slot buried beneath a roadway. When the operator of a car running on street-level tracks wanted to move his vehicle forward, he'd mechanically grip the cable with what's essentially a giant pair of pliers. To stop, the cable would be released and the brakes applied.

Even the naysayers were compelled to admit that they'd misjudged Hallidie as he piloted his tiny car along Clay Street that first day. He'd found a sturdy, mechanical way to surmount the steep hillslopes that had for so long daunted San Francisco's "hay burners" (horsecars). And his cable cars could carry more passengers than their predecessors. The future had arrived.

By 1878, three San Francisco cable railroads were in operation. During that same year, railroad magnate Leland Stanford sponsored construction of a first-class line up California Street—not so that he and other Nob Hill tycoons could ride the open-air cars to their mansions, but in hopes that this improved access would escalate property values on the higher slopes. At the apex of the system's popularity, in the late 1880s, some 600 cable cars crisscrossed this town with more than 110 miles of track, carrying passengers to their homes and businesses at a modest 9.5 miles an hour and encouraging the establishment of new residential developments in what had previously been remote locales such as the Western Addition and the Mission-Castro area. Unfortunately, these vehicles soon began succumbing to the encroachment of another new technology—electric trolleys. The system's decline was exacerbated by the earthquake and fire of 1906, which destroyed more than 100 cable cars and their power houses *(above)*.

After the city established its Municipal Railway (electric streetcar) system in 1912, there was a push to do away with the older cable vehicles. In 1942, the Clay Street line carried its final passenger. Five years later, Republican Mayor Roger Lapham envisioned their replacement by diesel-powered buses. A ballot referendum saved the Powell Street cars, but other cable lines weren't so lucky; the old Hyde Street "grip" cars were replaced by gas buses, despite protests *(left)*. However, in 1964, what remained of this city's cable-car system became America's first moving National Historic Monument. Tracks were rebuilt in the 1980s, and today's much-shrunken but still beloved system was relaunched.

PACIFIC HEIGHTS

The Bourn Mansion, at 2550 Webster Street, wouldn't look at all out of place in London, England. Yet it's a standout in Pacific Heights. Containing 28 rooms and more than a dozen fireplaces, this Georgian-style residence was constructed in 1896 for William Bourn II. Bourn had inherited the gold-rich Empire Mine in Grass Valley, California, after his father shot himself to death in 1874. He went on to accumulate fortunes of his own in real estate, electric and gas companies, and as president of the Spring Valley Water Company, which for a time was this city's principal water supplier. This brick mansion was designed by local architect Willis Polk. His work must have pleased Bourn immensely because he later hired Polk as chief designer of Filoli, his country estate south of the city, which is now a tourist attraction.

Haas-Lilienthal House

Even in a city recognized for its many Victorian homes, the Haas-Lilienthal house at 2007 Franklin Street holds special prominence. Designed by Bavarian architect Peter R. Schmidt, it was built in 1886 for the family of William Haas, a successful German Jewish grocer. The style is essentially Queen Anne, which was popular during America's Gilded Age. The house was threatened during the 1906 fire, but it survived while grander abodes along Van Ness Avenue did not. Three generations of the Haas and Lilienthal families occupied this residence. In 1972, it was donated to the Foundation for San Francisco's Architectural Heritage, which now offers public tours of the property.

Spreckels Mansion

Five years after marrying Adolph Spreckels, the heir to his father Claus's sugar empire, the former Alma de Bretteville supervised the design and construction of this white limestone, neoclassical château in Pacific Heights right off Lafayette Park. It was completed in 1913 according to plans by architect George Applegarth, a graduate of Paris's École des Beaux-Arts, who would later create the California Palace of the Legion of Honor on Mrs. Spreckels's behalf. This "Parthenon of the West," as it's often been called, demonstrated Alma's tastes in art. It also indicates the excesses of San Francisco's early 20th century millionaires, with its Tiffany glass ceiling over the entry hall, Louis XVI ballroom, giant fireplace flanked by Nubian slave figures, and cherubs kicking about in a Pompeian court. Over the decades, the Spreckels estate has appeared as a nightclub in Frank Sinatra's 1957 film *Pal Joey* and as a politician's residence in the 1968 Steve McQueen movie *Bullitt*. Best-selling novelist Danielle Steel bought the mansion in 1990.

RUSSIAN HILL

When it comes to houses with unexpected histories, this one is a standout. Located near the summit of Russian Hill at 1001 Vallejo Street, it was constructed in 1906 by Robert G. Hanford. He was a wealthy mining promoter and investor in railways and real estate. The architect was Houghton Sawyer, who also created other houses and apartment buildings in the Pacific Heights-Nob Hill area. As the story goes, Hanford built this Tudor-accented residence for Gabrielle Guittard Cavalsky, of the local Guittard chocolate-making family. Hanford met Gabrielle at a golf course in Monterey, California, and later left his wife for her. Unfortunately, the subsequent marriage didn't last long, and the residence changed hands repeatedly after their separation. It was once owned by Paul Verdier, a descendant of the family that founded downtown's City of Paris department store, and then became the abode of Sally Stanford, the long-time bordello owner and restaurateur who was elected mayor of Sausalito in the 1970s. During World War II, the house served as an officers' club, was later divided into apartments, and for many years suffered in poor condition (shown here in the mid to late 1900s). It was restored in the 1990s and became the home of Nobel Prize–winning economist Myron Scholes.

House of the Flag

This First Bay Tradition–style house, built during the 1860s at Vallejo and Taylor streets adjacent to Ina Coolbrith Park, is called the "House of the Flag" (left, circa 1906). And with good reason. It's said that just before evacuating this residence, one step ahead of the 1906 fire, its owner raised an American flag over his roof as a last act of defiance. Seeing that banner, soldiers from the 20th Infantry Regiment, who had recently returned from the Philippines and were enlisted to help battle the blaze, rushed to the site. Using water extracted from the home's bathtubs, seltzer bottles, and sodden sand from a construction site nearby, they saved the house from ruin and protected others on the surrounding hillslopes.

San Francisco Art Institute

The San Francisco Art Association (SFAA) was founded in 1871, and it opened its School of Design in 1874. Both came to prominence in the 1890s, when the school and museum facilities moved into the former Mark Hopkins manor atop Nob Hill. Following the 1906 disaster, the SFAA constructed a new home on the Hopkins site. But a decade later, it took over the grand Palace of Fine Arts, a relic of the 1915 Panama-Pacific International Exposition in the Marina District. Not until 1926 did the school move to its present location at 800 Chestnut Street (above, in 1927). This Mediterranean-style edifice was designed by Arthur Brown, Jr., and John Bakewell, who had also created San Francisco's City Hall. The school adopted its modern name, the San Francisco Art Institute (SFAI), in 1961. In 1970, work was completed on a Le Corbusier–influenced addition to the institute, designed by British-born local architect Paffard Keatinge-Clay.

CUT TO THE CHASE

PERHAPS THE GREATEST movie car-chase scene of all time was shot largely on Russian Hill. It's the 9 minute, 42 second centerpiece of actor Steve McQueen's 1968 thriller *Bullitt*. Through the wonders of cinema-tography, the high-speed, tire-squealing pursuit—pitting McQueen in his own Mustang Fastback against a Dodge Charger driven by a couple of bad guys—takes the cars all over San Francisco. It begins in the Bernal Heights area, quickly transfers onto Potrero Hill, then skips several miles north to Russian Hill and North Beach. Prior to *Bullitt*, car-chase scenes were usually shot at slower speeds and then sped up in the studio to increase their drama. This movie established a new, riskier standard.

LOMBARD STREET

For local teenagers with new driver's licenses, steering their cars down steep, twisting Lombard Street on the north side of Russian Hill has long been a rite of passage. Don't take your foot off the brake, don't run into any flower beds or pedestrians, and you should be fine. Long promoted as the most crooked thoroughfare in San Francisco (a claim challenged by a short segment of Vermont Street between 20th and 22nd streets in the Potrero Hill neighborhood), the stretch of Lombard from Hyde down to Leavenworth comprises eight brick-paved switchbacks over the distance of a single city block. Its design was proposed by adjacent property owner Carl A. Henry, an executive at the old Owl Drug Company, as a means of reducing the 27-degree grade of this slope to a more reasonable 17-degree driving incline. The serpentine roadway—part of much longer Lombard Street, which cuts from the Presidio east to North Beach—was built in 1922 *(top)*. But it wasn't until the 1960s that it became celebrated, thanks to postcards bearing its likeness. Suddenly, every tourist in town wanted to negotiate this attraction. Neighbors, upset at the rising traffic congestion and noise, petitioned the city to close this bit of Lombard, but that idea failed. You could say that things have been going downhill ever since. *Bottom:* Lombard Street as it appeared in 1933, when it was still a quiet stretch of concrete.

This one-way street has been featured in video games as well as in one of comedian Bill Cosby's best-known sketches, "Driving in San Francisco," where the comic muses about driving down the bends of the risky thoroughfare. Although it's renowned for its twists, this length of Lombard also offers spectacular views of Alcatraz Island and the Gold Gate.

Mrs. Robert Louis Stevenson Home

Not all of crooked Lombard's significance is contained in its curves. At the top of this hill, at 2319–2323 Hyde Street, can be seen a four-story, Mediterranean villa–style construction that was once the home of Fanny Osbourne Stevenson, the widow of renowned 19th-century Scottish novelist Robert Louis Stevenson. It was designed for her by architect Willis Polk. (Just behind Fanny's mansion, Polk created a second home at 1100 Lombard Street. This house was for her son, author Lloyd Osbourne.) Fanny's residence originally stood only two stories high and had the appearance more of a Tudor-Baroque manor than a Mediterranean villa. After she moved out, new owners enlarged the structure, and for a time, it served as a convent.

Living on the Edge

Until the first transcontinental railway steamed into Northern California after the Civil War, most settlers and opportunists arrived in this area by sea. That included the tens of thousands who came for the gold rush, men so impatient to milk the mother lode that they never looked back to see what became of the craft that had brought them here. The fact is, many of the ships never made it out of Yerba Buena Cove, their crews abandoning them in order to follow the forty-niners into the Sierra foothills. By 1851, about 775 deserted sailboats crowded the Bay, their creaking, skeletal masts giving the impression of a forest afloat.

Many of these stranded ships were simply left to rot and sink, or they were destroyed during the town's early fires, becoming part of the fill that eventually eliminated Yerba Buena Cove and created today's Embarcadero.

SUCCESS AT SEA

At the same time the ocean provided entry to this boomtown's populace, it also gave San Francisco the hope of commercial prosperity. Even before the sun rose most mornings, fishers would set out in tiny sailboats to gather tuna, crab, and other seafood. For decades, the city's fishing industry thrived, despite rivalries between folks involved in the enterprise. Shipping, too, has long been crucial to the local economy. During the late 19th and early 20th centuries, this city dominated the West Coast maritime trade. To accommodate the torrent of vessels, wooden wharves fingered out into the Bay from the city's northern edge—many of them small, others large and infamous, such as Meiggs Wharf and McMahon's Wharf. Most shipping facilities are now centered around China Basin south of Market Street, though recreational boating, sport fishing, and cruise-ship facilities can still be found on the touristy northern waterfront.

PROTECTING LAND AND SEA

If there was a downside to San Francisco being surrounded by water, it was that this left the city vulnerable to seagoing attack. In 1850, the U.S. Army and Navy jointly recommended raising a necklace of defensive installations around the Bay. Only some of those were built, including Fort Point at the narrowest part of the Golden Gate, a stronghold on Alcatraz Island (later leveled to make room for the federal penitentiary), and Fort Mason at what used to be known

Female soldiers, or "soldierettes," in training at the Presidio military base in 1916. It is unknown whether these women came anywhere close to the trenches of World War I.

Left: The remains of neglected ships sat in Yerba Buena Cove in the mid-1850s, as their owners headed out to reap the benefits of the gold rush.

Top: A couple takes a stroll on "Travelers Day" at the Panama-Pacific International Exposition in 1915.
Bottom: A souvenir booklet from the Exposition.

as Black Point. Meanwhile, the historic Presidio was revamped and armed more heavily than before.

None of these redoubts proved essential to the city's protection, but they lent it a sense of permanence and left it with landmarks that help define its significance to U.S. history.

TOURISM ON THE WATER

Best known of those remains is Alcatraz. The Spanish name *La Isla de los Alcatraces,* referring either to the presence of cormorants (*alcatraceo*) or pelicans (*alcaraz*), may have been applied originally to what's now tiny Yerba Buena Island. But an English mapmaker in the 1820s is said to have mistakenly lashed that moniker to the once smooth expanse of Alcatraz east of the Golden Gate. From the time it began hosting gangsters and other "public enemies" in 1934, Alcatraz earned a reputation as a hellhole amid the heavenly surroundings of San Francisco Bay. Given the often harsh conditions prevailing there, it's hardly surprising that escape attempts were made and violence erupted. Yet it was not until 1963 that Alcatraz was closed, mainly because it was too costly to operate. The 22-acre island is now part of the Golden Gate Recreation Area and receives more than a million visitors every year.

Most of the waterfront boasts no such notoriety. Fisherman's Wharf swarms with tourists hungry for clam chowder in sourdough bread bowls, military buffs wander the barracks and long-ago reforested reaches of the Presidio, coeds play catch on the sunlit lawn at the Marina Green (created in the 1920s by Golden Gate Park designer John McLaren), and photographers take sightings on the steel passageway of the Golden Gate Bridge.

The Marina District, so damaged by the 1989 Loma Prieta earthquake, again welcomes strollers among its art deco and Mediterranean Revival homes. It was in the Marina District that the 1915 Panama-Pacific International Exposition was held—the last classically themed world's fair in America. After beating New Orleans for the privilege of holding the expo, San Francisco created an extravaganza so big, flashy, and fun-loving that visitors forgot it was all an expensive stage set. After the fair was torn down, grand plans were made for the Marina District's development. But the site remained vacant until the 1920s, save for a landing strip employed by airmail planes and the fair's once lauded Column of Progress. This pillar remained a lonely and increasingly anachronistic fixture on the north waterfront, until it was finally removed a decade after the fair's closing to accommodate automobiles traveling Marina Boulevard.

Drive that boulevard today and you'll see the broad expanse of the Golden Gate—the waterway through which so many gold seekers, immigrants, gamblers, ramblers, and good-time girls came to this distant spot on the frontier more than a century and a half ago.

Today, residents of the Marina District get a view of both sailboats huddled on the waterfront and afternoon promenaders.

Fisherman's Wharf, 1912

FISHERMAN'S WHARF

San Francisco's waterfront has historically provided a vigorous concentration of commerce, even if it hasn't always boasted quite so many seafood stands, souvenir shops, and other tourist entertainments as it does today. During the gold rush, the docks were hectic with ships tying up and unloading passengers or cargo. Later, woolen mills, packinghouses, and imposing brick warehouses marched north from the eastern terminus of Market Street, along what was then known as East Street (now the Embarcadero). But piers were also lively with fishers, many of whom had arrived in California from Italy—particularly Genoa and Sicily. They quickly established themselves as the principal providers of seafood to local tables. At one time, this city's sail-driven fishing fleet launched from points all along the waterfront, including piers at North Beach. However, around 1900, as work on the seawall (which had begun in 1878) was finally winding down, the hardy, sunburned souls who made their living off the ocean's plenitude were relocated to what is now Fisherman's Wharf.

Meiggs Wharf

While Fisherman's Wharf is now the harbor's foremost draw, it was preceded by a no-less-eccentric attraction: Meiggs Wharf (left, in 1866). Built in 1853, it extended more than 1,600 feet out into the Bay, from a point on the original North Beach shoreline near the present intersection of Francisco and Powell streets. It was named for "Honest Harry" Meiggs, a former New York lumberman who, after shipping west in 1849, invested heavily in local real estate, bought sawmills, and laid roads through North Beach that he hoped would enhance the value of his holdings. However, not long after the wharf's completion, Honest Harry fled to South America after defrauding his creditors and the city of San Francisco out of hundreds of thousands of dollars. The far end of Meiggs Wharf, which was eventually buried beneath landfill, lies near today's Embarcadero.

Abe Warner's Cobweb Palace

Although Meiggs built his immense, L-shape pier primarily to serve the lumber trade, it took on another life as an amusement center. There was a shooting gallery, a stand where folks tried to climb a greased pole and nab a $5 gold piece at the top, and Cockney White's museum, famous for its "educated pig" that played card games. And at the shore end was Abe Warner's Cobweb Palace. A bar and eatery specializing in clam chowder, it was stocked from floor to ceiling with oddities—scrimshaw made from sperm-whale teeth; South Pacific war clubs; Alaskan totem poles; and a caged menagerie of monkeys, kangaroos, and parrots—along with myriad drooping spiderwebs. The interior is shown here in the mid-1800s, with Abe himself sporting his signature top hat.

It wasn't until after 1906 that Fisherman's Wharf started to pull in substantial numbers of tourists. However, San Francisco's fishing industry became less vital even as the number of visitors increased. The Bay's bounty was heavily depleted during the 20th century, and pollution threatened what remained. Restaurants, chowder houses, and crab stands (shown above in 1946) became the focus as fishing boats disappeared. The Bay is still harvested for Dungeness crab, sardines, and other seafood, but most Fisherman's Wharf visitors see little of that activity today.

Fishermen's Grotto and DiMaggio's Restaurant

Wherever tourists go, restaurants follow. That's certainly been the case along Fisherman's Wharf. One of the earliest popular dining spots was Alioto's, which started as a fish stall opened by Sicilian immigrants Nunzio and Rose Alioto in 1925. The Aliotos expanded their stand in 1932 to include a seafood bar, and you can still purchase cracked crab on the sidewalk there today. Located nearby is Fishermen's Grotto (shown at right in 1939), founded in 1935 by Mike Geraldi, who as a tyke had gone door-to-door peddling seafood he had received in exchange for helping fishers unload their catches. And though it was shuttered in the 1980s, DiMaggio's was also once a Wharf landmark. It was launched in 1937 by the local-boy-turned-baseball-star and his brothers, all of whom had been reared in the area by their immigrant fisherman father. It was here that "Joltin' Joe" brought his new bride, Marilyn Monroe, after their City Hall marriage in 1954.

A menu from the "world famous" DiMaggio's

GHIRARDELLI SQUARE

Italian chocolatier Domenico "Domingo" Ghirardelli came to California during the gold rush hoping to strike it rich. But after failing at mining and seeing a hotel he'd constructed burn down during San Francisco's 1851 fire, he returned to what he knew best, chocolate making, and opened a confectionery company in 1852. Four decades later, Domingo turned his now-thriving enterprise over to his three sons, who in 1893 bought the former Pioneer Woolen Mill on North Point Street and turned it into a candy factory (right, in the mid-1800s). That mill had been designed in the late 1850s or early '60s by Swiss-born architect William Mooser, and the younger Ghirardellis wisely hired his son, William Mooser II (later to be tapped as San Francisco's first city architect), to develop a manufacturing complex that incorporated the mill. Work on the plant—including a 1916 clock tower said to have been modeled after a French château at Blois—continued into the early 1920s. The giant electric Ghirardelli sign dates to 1926 (below).

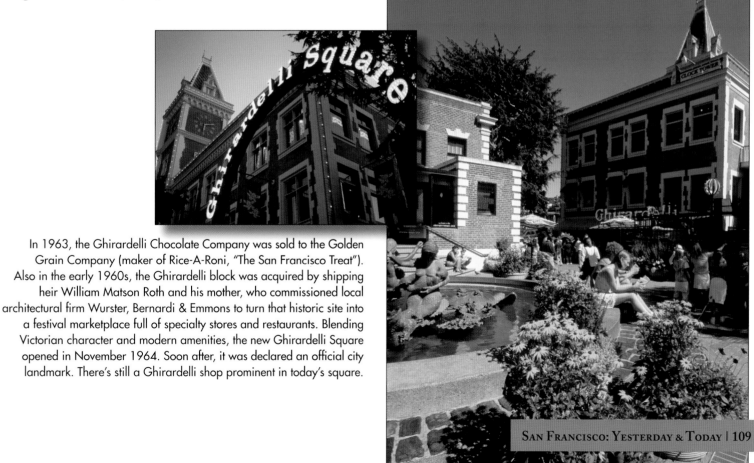

In 1963, the Ghirardelli Chocolate Company was sold to the Golden Grain Company (maker of Rice-A-Roni, "The San Francisco Treat"). Also in the early 1960s, the Ghirardelli block was acquired by shipping heir William Matson Roth and his mother, who commissioned local architectural firm Wurster, Bernardi & Emmons to turn that historic site into a festival marketplace full of specialty stores and restaurants. Blending Victorian character and modern amenities, the new Ghirardelli Square opened in November 1964. Soon after, it was declared an official city landmark. There's still a Ghirardelli shop prominent in today's square.

ALCATRAZ ISLAND

Hoping to avoid navigational calamities as ships crowded into San Francisco Bay during the gold rush, Congress approved the construction of a lighthouse on Alcatraz Island—the first such American installation on the West Coast. Meanwhile, this craggy outcropping was designated as one of several spots around the Bay where military strongholds should be erected. By 1861, when the Civil War erupted, there were some 100 cannons on the island *(top)*, but they were fired only once in a threatening manner, after a British vessel entered the Bay without following proper protocol. It wasn't long before Alcatraz began accepting military prisoners, many of them Confederate sympathizers, and its citadel was replaced by detention stockades. Later, soldiers who had contracted tropical diseases while fighting in the Philippines were quarantined here, and malcontents were shipped over after the 1906 earthquake destroyed San Francisco jails. In 1907, Alcatraz officially became a military prison, the grumbling of inmates and barked orders of guards contrasting sharply with the peace and quiet enjoyed by the dozens of families of prison employees who also lived on the island. *Bottom:* Alcatraz Island before it became a military prison, circa the 1890s.

With crime on the rise nationwide thanks to the Great Depression and Prohibition, in 1934 the U.S. Bureau of Prisons took control of Alcatraz and turned it into a maximum security penitentiary—a place to which the most violent lawbreakers could be sent and from which any escape was expected to be foiled by the frigid clutch of the Bay. Among the "public enemies" confined to "the Rock" were Chicago gang leader Al "Scarface" Capone; murderer Robert Stroud, better remembered as "the Birdman of Alcatraz"; and bank-robbing brothers John and Clarence Anglin. Along with armed robber Frank Morris, the brothers slowly dug through their cell walls and escaped Alcatraz on a raft in 1962, never to be recaptured. However, bits of raft and their personal effects were later found in the Bay, leading to suspicions that they had drowned. That adventure inspired Clint Eastwood's 1979 film, *Escape from Alcatraz.*

Released convict Bryan Conway said, "Men slowly go insane under the exquisite torture of routine." Silence was enforced within Alcatraz's walls, with inmates locked in single cells. Gifts from the outside were forbidden. Visitors were permitted once a month, although no physical contact was allowed. Lonely convicts made pets of mice, feeding them bread they filched at mealtime, risking being tossed into solitary confinement. Alcatraz today is open to visitors wishing to view the bone-chilling sights of the former penitentiary. An audio tour of the prison cells *(left)* gives details about inmate treatment and escape attempts.

PANAMA-PACIFIC EXPO

The Panama-Pacific International Exposition opened on February 20, 1915, and ran for the next ten months, welcoming 18 million visitors. It was situated on 635 acres in what had been a marshy and lagoon-ridden outlying sector of the city north of Cow Hollow called Harbor View—today's Marina District. The challenge for this fair's chief of architecture, George W. Kelham (who'd supervised construction of the second Palace Hotel and would go on to create the original main library at Civic Center), was to give San Francisco a fair that not only brought a bit of the world to the Bay Area but showed the world that this recently ruined burg had been rebuilt and revitalized and was open for business again. He drew on the talents of local designers such as Willis Polk, Louis Mullgardt, and Bernard Maybeck and created a Beaux Arts–style fanta-syland that looked permanent but was shaped from imitation travertine made of gypsum, hemp fiber, and plaster. *Right:* the fair's centerpiece was the 435-foot-tall Italianate Tower of Jewels, on which sparkled tens of thousands of "nova-gems," polished cut-glass "jewels" that were strung along the edifice and backed by bits of mirror to increase their reflections. On the left and down the Avenue of Palms is the glass-domed Palace of Horticulture.

Souvenir opening and closing day badges commemorate the Exposition, which celebrated the opening of the Panama Canal.

Creation

Contrasting with the seriousness of the main fair, "The Zone"—stretching east from Fillmore Street to Van Ness Avenue and south of Fort Mason—sought to amuse as well as amaze. Among this midway's attractions were a five-acre working model of the Panama Canal, Pueblo and Samoan villages, an ostrich farm, reproductions of the Grand Canyon and the Old Faithful Inn, performances by divers and bullfighters, infant incubators demonstrating how weak babies could be made healthier, and the Aerospace, a mechanical arm that lifted carloads of passengers 285 feet into the air for an unsurpassed view of the Exposition. The Zone also contained *Creation*, its facade decorated with mammals, a topless angel, and lightning-filled storm clouds, while inside electric light effects and a colorful tableau dramatized the Book of Genesis.

Japan Pavilion

Everywhere one roamed within the fairgrounds there was something—usually monumental in scale—to attract the eye, be it the main exhibition buildings (celebrating American industry and ingenuity), courtyards landscaped by Golden Gate Park developer John McLaren, or the international and state pavilions, which stretched west into the Presidio. Forty-six U.S. states and territories contributed exhibits to this site, including a Spanish mission–style California Building with seven bell towers, and the Oregon Building, a Parthenon reproduction shaped of old-growth logs. There were also 31 foreign nations participating, among them Cuba, Portugal, Siam, Sweden, and Argentina. Great Britain, which was busy fending off early World War I German bombardments at home, was noticeably absent. Japan's Golden Pavilion *(right)* replicated a classic Japanese temple and was encircled by three acres of gardens, teahouses, and imported rocks.

PALACE OF FINE ARTS

If the 1915 fair impressed visitors with its architecture, it did no less so with its abundance of art. Renowned Philadelphia sculptor A. Stirling Calder (the father of artist and mobile inventor Alexander Calder) had been recruited to fill this site with more than 1,500 sculptures from around the globe. Some, such as James Earle Fraser's representation of a dying Indian on a horse (*End of the Trail*), were displayed conspicuously, while others took a secondary role as decoration or were placed to surprise in corners of the campus. An example of that last breed was *Wind and Spray,* Anna Coleman Ladd's circle of dancing, nude female and male figures that rose from the lagoon at the Palace of Fine Arts. A Massachusetts sculptress, Ladd exhibited a dozen pieces at the Panama-Pacific Exposition before going on to unexpected fame creating metal noses and fuller "portrait masks" for soldiers who had suffered severe facial damage in World War I. *Wind and Spray* earned a fond following in San Francisco, but when it was later moved to Boston's Public Garden, its nakedness kicked up such controversy that it was removed from public display.

The sculpture *Wind and Spray (foreground)* is displayed at the lagoon of the Palace of Fine Arts during the Expo.

Entry tickets for the Palace of Fine Arts on "San Francisco Day" at the Exposition

Star Maiden

Artist A. Stirling Calder created many sculptures for the fair, including his ubiquitous *Star Maiden*, modeled after Audrey Munson, a prominent young New Yorker of the era who also inspired some three-quarters of the fair's female figures. Nearly 100 of these maidens lined the upper balustrade of the Court of the Universe, but she also appeared in the Exposition's insignia and on its official engravings.

Willis Polk had originally been slated to design the Palace of Fine Arts on the fair's west side. But instead he generously handed that commission over to an elder mentor, Bernard Maybeck, who'd been working as a draftsman in Polk's office. Maybeck created a classical rotunda, a sweeping colonnade, and an exhibition hall beside a reflecting lagoon—a much-needed place of nature and relaxation amid the surrounding frenzy. So beloved was it that when the rest of the fairgrounds were leveled, Maybeck's masterpiece remained. Unfortunately, its construction in ersatz travertine didn't hold up to weather and age. After years of deterioration, the Palace of Fine Arts was demolished and rebuilt in the late 1960s, this time of concrete, but it lost some of its decorative features in the process. Its exhibition hall now contains the Exploratorium, a popular public science museum.

MARINA DISTRICT

Orson Squire Fowler was a 19th-century New York author and lecturer on the pseudoscience of phrenology, which argued that human characteristics, including personality and criminal traits, could be determined by studying the contours of a person's head. He also promoted the construction of octagon-shape houses, which he contended were less expensive to build, invited more natural light, and stayed cooler in warm weather (a valuable trait in the age before air conditioning). Local miller William McElroy took Fowler's architectural advice when he constructed his two-story, cupola-topped home in 1861 (pictured above in 1906). Known by schoolchildren as "the Inkwell House," it originally stood on the east side of Gough Street at Union, but in the 1950s it was purchased by the National Society of Colonial Dames of America and moved across Gough to its present location. It's now a museum of decorative arts.

Vedanta Temple

Architecture's underappreciated capacity for whimsy is well-expressed in the Vedanta Temple at Webster and Filbert streets. Built in 1905, it was created by Joseph A. Leonard, a Texas-born, New York-trained designer and developer whose best-recognized legacy may be Ingleside Terraces, one of San Francisco's first "residence parks." The Temple's confection of Edwardian, Queen Anne, and Oriental styles, festooned with onion domes and a Moorish arcade, was supposed to symbolize the inclusive nature of Vedanta, the philosophical foundation of Hinduism. The building has been described as "a meeting of the mysterious East and the uninhibited West."

North of the Marina Green you'll find architect Willis Polk's Mediterranean Revival–style St. Francis Yacht Club, constructed in 1928. And east of there is this stone lighthouse, dating to 1931. Although it no longer operates as a beacon, it remains a landmark for visitors seeking the adjacent Wave Organ, a quirky construction of underwater tubes, built by scientists from the Exploratorium, that projects the sound of the changing tides.

THE PRESIDIO

In 1850, President Millard Fillmore determined that the U.S. military should assume control over all the coastline stretching from what's now Fisherman's Wharf to the promontory at Lands End on the Pacific—about 10,000 acres. Land speculators, however, balked at the tops of their lungs. So Fillmore scaled back his request, asking for about 2,500 acres around the old Spanish-Mexican Presidio. During the Civil War, Union regiments trained there, even though the battle never reached California. Later, the Presidio supplied artillery units to help suppress Native American uprisings across the West. And throughout the Spanish-American War it served as the West Coast's chief recruitment post, sending tens of thousands of soldiers to the Philippines. After the 1906 earthquake and fire, the Presidio became a refugee camp, housing the hurt and homeless. And during World War II it served as the center of army operations for the Western United States. After that war, President Harry Truman proposed that the United Nations establish its headquarters at the Presidio, but the Soviet Union rejected the offer.

In addition to housing and training soldiers, the Presidio was where the sick and wounded were cared for in the 20th century. The U.S. Army General Hospital was originally established in the final years of the 19th century to deal with the health problems of 20,000 troops assembling at Camp Merritt (shown above in 1898), a temporary housing for men headed to the Philippines during the Spanish-American War. In 1911, the facility (at right in the early 1900s) was renamed for Major Jonathan Letterman, a surgeon and former medical director of the Army of the Potomac, who significantly improved battlefield-care procedures during the Civil War. Seven years later, Letterman Army Hospital was the army's largest such facility. The original hospital was replaced by a more modern one during the Vietnam War, but the Thoreau Center for Sustainability took over the dilapidated Letterman Hospital buildings after the army decommissioned the Presidio in 1994. More recently, director-producer George Lucas's production company, Lucasfilm Limited, redeveloped 23 acres of the hospital site as the Letterman Digital Arts Center.

There were once many cemeteries in this city, containing tens of thousands of the dearly departed. But in the early 1900s, the Board of Supervisors—wanting to preserve valuable real estate for the living rather than the dead—forbade further interments from taking place within the city, and soon after they evicted existing cemeteries. However, four sites remain: the charnel next to Mission Dolores, Richmond's Columbarium of San Francisco, a columbarium inside Grace Cathedral, and the Presidio's San Francisco National Cemetery. The last site, created in 1884, now holds more than 30,000 graves, including three dozen Congressional Medal of Honor winners. *Top:* The pet cemetery at the Presidio. *Bottom:* Women laying flowers on graves on Memorial Day 1942.

After more than two centuries, the Presidio's role as a military post came to a close in the early 1990s, when the army finally moved out. It's now a National Historic Landmark District and part of the Golden Gate National Recreation Area, a giant necklace of preserved sites ringing San Francisco Bay. Managed by the Presidio Trust, a nonprofit organization charged with making it financially self-sufficient, the Presidio has become a favorite spot for military history buffs, bicyclists, nature lovers, and strollers along the Golden Gate Promenade, which leads all the way to Fort Point, beneath the Golden Gate Bridge.

Fort Point, 1911

FORT POINT

Interestingly, the name "Golden Gate" was not applied to the opposing headlands of the San Francisco Peninsula and the Marin Peninsula as a consequence of the area's abundant riches. Instead, it is said that John C. Frémont, the 19th-century explorer and onetime military governor of California, named the three-mile-long passage "Chrysopylae," or Golden Gate, because it reminded him of a waterway bisecting the Ottoman (Turkish) city of Constantinople (Istanbul) called "Chrysoceras," or Golden

Horn. Although ships from England and Spain had sailed past this 6,700-foot-wide strait for two centuries, the first recorded European sighting dates only to November 1769, when a Spanish scouting party from Mexico was stopped in its northward march by the channel. Recognizing the site's strategic importance, Spain planned a fortress at the narrowest part of the entrance to San Francisco Bay. But the Spaniards built nothing there until after 1792, when British Captain George Vancouver piloted his

sloop-of-war *Discovery* through the inlet, unchallenged, to call at the Presidio. The new Spanish citadel, though, wasn't adequate to its task. "Munitions were in such short supply," Rand Richards wrote in his book *Historic San Francisco*, "that when, in 1806, a Russian ship entered the bay and fired a friendly salute, the Spanish soldiers had to row out to the vessel to borrow enough powder to fire a return salute." Fifty-five years later, the U.S. Army completed Fort Point on the same promontory.

The first and only American installation of its kind west of the Mississippi River, Fort Point was built between 1853 and 1861 to guard the Bay from ocean-borne attack. The outcropping on which it rests was once about 100 feet high, but it was blasted down by the U.S. Army to a height of approximately 15 feet so that the fortress's lowest level of artillery would be near sea level, making it possible to skip cannonballs across the water at enemy ships. Toward the end of the 19th century, Fort Point (above, circa late 1800s) was disarmed and plans were made to either demolish it or turn it into a military detention center—both fates from which it was ultimately spared.

The fort again faced the prospect of destruction during the planning of the Golden Gate Bridge. It sat where the bridge's southern anchorage was supposed to go. After visiting the old brick-and-mortar citadel, however, chief engineer Joseph Strauss determined that he would build around it instead; further, he suggested that Fort Point be preserved and restored as a national monument. Following the efforts of a public support campaign, in 1970 the fort became a National Historic Site. It's now administered by the National Park Service as part of the Golden Gate National Recreation Area and is open to the public.

THE FOGGIEST NOTIONS

- It's said that San Francisco has three seasons: winter, summer, and fog. The city gets the vapors every summer, when the sun heats up the Sacramento and San Joaquin valleys, and cool, foggy ocean air is sucked eastward through the Golden Gate. The fog stops when the Central Valley cools, only to repeat this cycle as the mists burn off and temperatures there climb again. Winter's notorious tule fog is a sort of conga line formed by low-hanging clouds of condensed vapor that weave about the Bay, completely overwhelming one district while others enjoy sunshine.

- According to the *San Francisco Chronicle,* "In 1968, [local author and environmentalist] Harold Gilliam identified nine different summer fog formations: wreaths and domes over Alcatraz; arches over the Golden Gate Bridge; eddies and fog falls that look like cascades over Twin Peaks in San Francisco and the Sausalito hills; surges and combers over the peninsula and past the top of the hill in Daly City; rivers of fog at places like Candlestick Park; and the so-called fog decks, where fingers of fog skip over the bay and into Berkeley."

- Robert Louis Stevenson celebrated "the fog...rising over the c00. citied hills" when he first visited San Francisco in 1879. Entranced, too, was early 20th-century poet George Sterling, who in verse dubbed this the "cool, grey city of love." And Dashiell Hammett turned the fog into a minor character in *The Maltese Falcon,* calling it "thin, clammy, and penetrant."

- During the Golden Gate Bridge's construction in 1933, a drizzle-laden haze caused the freighter *Sidney M. Hauptman,* outbound for Portland, Oregon, to smash into a construction access trestle with enough force that the bow was crushed and a 120-foot section of the trestle was knocked clean away.

- While playing golf at an oceanside course decades ago, New York fashion maven Alvin Handmacher stared out from San Francisco into a solid wall of gray. "So that's the Pacific Ocean," he quipped. "They told me it was much bigger."

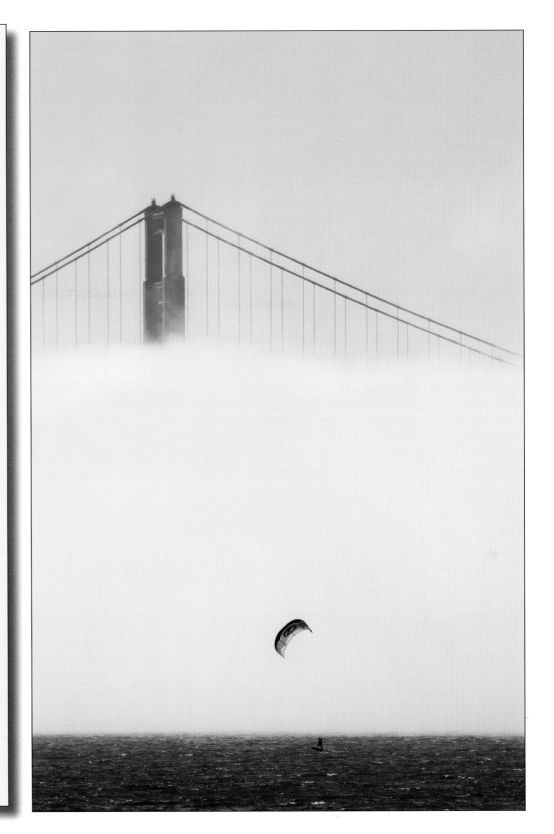

Fog sweeps in the Golden Gate to cool the city in 1949.

GOLDEN GATE BRIDGE

Prior to construction of the Golden Gate Bridge in the 1930s, a profitable ferry service (dating to the mid-19th century) carried passengers—and later automobiles as well—from San Francisco to Marin County, a 20-minute trip. There had been talk for decades about bridging the scenic gap between San Francisco Bay and the Pacific Ocean, a channel that had been cut over millennia by the outflow of seven different rivers. But it was deemed an impossible engineering feat, the Gate being too wide (more than a mile, even at its narrowest point), too deep (335 feet at its center), and too treacherous (with tides and mammoth ocean waves) to allow for construction. Following World War I, though, Midwestern engineer Joseph Strauss contended that not only could he design such a span, but he could build it for just over $17 million—less than a tenth of previous estimates. Unfortunately, his original concept resembled an overgrown railroad bridge, ugly and bluntly functional *(illustrated above).*

Fortunately, Strauss abandoned his original part-suspension, part-cantilever design in favor of today's more graceful cable suspension span. It was created in large part by Charles Ellis, a professor of structural and bridge engineering at the University of Illinois whom Strauss later fired, and architect Irving Morrow. Construction commenced in January 1933, and it took four years to finish. During the building, 11 men died and enough concrete was poured to have laid a five-foot-wide road all the way from San Francisco to New York City. At the time of its completion, the Golden Gate Bridge was the world's longest and tallest suspension structure, and it remains one of the ten longest single-span bridges. It also cost about $35 million to complete—twice what Strauss had originally estimated. *Above:* Workers braved the heights in 1935.

Grand Opening

On the morning of Thursday, May 27, 1937—a day before traffic was welcomed onto the bridge—pedestrians were allowed to cross its 8,981-foot length. Local schools were closed in celebration, and many office workers took the day off. When the barriers dropped, the earliest arrivals walked onto the span. Or, in the case of these three celebrants, they skated, hoping to become the first to cross. Two hundred thousand people went over the bridge that day, some of them tap-dancing, unicycling, and stilt-walking its length.

The U.S. Department of the Navy asked that San Francisco's new bridge be painted with yellow and black stripes to increase its visibility, especially in fog. Chief engineer Strauss wanted it to be solid black so it wouldn't show dirt. But architect Morrow won out, choosing an orange vermillion hue (called "International Orange") that makes the structure stand out against the sky and water yet is warm enough to blend well with the land masses on either end. No local landmark is more loved and more synonymous with San Francisco than this bridge. When, in the wake of the terrorist attacks on New York City and Washington, D.C., in 2001, reports circulated that the Golden Gate might be the next target, you could almost hear the nation gasp in shock. Thankfully, nothing came of such threats.

A view of Rincon Hill from the south in 1870

"The Heart of the City Is South o' the Slot"

For the majority of today's tourists, San Francisco only exists north of Market Street. South of the city's principal east-west thoroughfare is pretty much terra incognita. In recent years, efforts have been made to attract both visitors and wary locals into the South of Market area (or SoMa, as neighborhood touts refer to it). This quarter now hosts the exquisite San Francisco Museum of Modern Art (SFMOMA), together with the Moscone Convention Center, named in memory of the town's long-ago murdered mayor, and adjacent Yerba Buena Gardens. Still farther south, right on the scenic edge of the Bay, there's AT&T Park, home of the San Francisco Giants.

Yet even today, the SoMa district is often largely thought of as a place one drives *through*, rather than *to*. This hasn't always been the case. Many post–gold rush nouveaux riches and practiced plutocrats made their homes south of Market, where the climate was said to be warmer than in the north. They constructed garden-cuddled mansions atop Rincon Hill, overlooking old Yerba Buena Cove and just south of the Financial District, or bought row houses in the equally exclusive pocket of South Park. But this precinct's days as a prestigious address were numbered. In the late 1860s, John Middleton, a California state legislator who had arrived in the Bay Area with the forty-niners and hoped to augment the value of his property along Second Street, spearheaded a plan to lower Second's grade. This

would thereby make it easier for cargo wagons traveling south from downtown to reach the shipping wharves at South Beach. Unfortunately, it also resulted in a 100-foot-deep chasm being torn directly through Rincon Hill, from Folsom to Bryant streets, and a high cast-iron bridge being stretched across that "Second Street Cut" at Harrison. The area's better-off residents, already glum over the proliferation of clamorous factories throughout South of Market and neighboring Potrero Hill, took this excavation as a signal to move.

OF PRIDE & PROPERTY

Slowly but surely, immigrants from Europe and Asia stepped in to take their place. South of Market went from glamorous to working-class, its air pungent with the bouquet of

The "Second Street Cut," 1869

A panorama of South of Market, mid-1900s

industrialization, its thoroughfares becoming kinetic pageants of commerce. South of Market had lost its pretensions but gained a fiercely loyal populace, defiant of those who would disparage their home turf. The opening stanza of a poem once popular in this neighborhood makes such pride plain:

Whether you know your locations or not,
The heart of the city is South o' the Slot!
That is the spot,
True to the dot—
The heart of the city is South o' the Slot.

"South of the Slot" referred to the cable-car tracks—the slots with their buried loops of steel rope—that were laid down Market Street in the 1880s. Old-timers still refer affectionately to this quarter as South of the Slot, as if it were a world away from the body of the city—which many people living here in 1906 prob-

ably wished it had been. The quake that hit in April of that year was particularly rough on South of Market. Streets that had been built over the old Mission Bay swamplands—Minna, Jessie, Matoma, and the rest (said to have been named after ex-girlfriends of mid-19th century surveyor Jasper O'Farrell)—suffered the most damage. After the disaster, many residents packed up and left for the Western Addition, not willing to risk more loss of property and life. The first part of the 20th century found South of the Slot economically depressed.

OF EXPOS & ISLANDS

Construction of the Bay Bridge in the mid-1930s resulted in the vestiges of once-dignified Rincon Hill being blasted away, leaving blocks of South of Market that lay beneath the span's western approaches in deep shadow. But it also brought union jobs and federal dollars.

The same was true of the building of Treasure Island a few years later. It was created immediately north of Yerba Buena Island using landfill dredged up from the Bay, on which was mounted the 1939–40 Golden Gate International Exposition—the third of San Francisco's world's fairs. World War II was a boon as well for this area, as workers came here in search of dockyard employment.

Since then, South of Market has been identified variously as a prominent gay hangout and an urban renewal zone. Only in recent years has it been rediscovered by youthful business entrepreneurs and white-collar workers who appreciate old warehouses and plentiful loft spaces, and by starter families who like the unusually clean streets of Potrero Hill. You see lots of new restaurants down there, and a scattering of fine old buildings that recall the precinct's glory days.

SOUTH OF MARKET

During the late 19th century, South of Market "consisted of factories, slums, laundries, machine shops, boiler works, and the abodes of the working class," as author Jack London, who was born on Third Street just off Rincon Hill, wrote in his 1909 short story "South of the Slot." While the area north of Market won the lion's share of attention and money, it was to a great extent the European immigrants living South of the Slot—the folks who ran the gasworks and shipbuilding docks, shopped in the German groceries, and drank in the Irish saloons—who really made this city run. By 1900, South of Market was the second most densely populated area of San Francisco after Chinatown, containing one-fifth of the city's inhabitants. As a result, the loss of life here was particularly heavy during the 1906 earthquake. The disaster played havoc with the unstable fill land and fire devoured the area's wooden structures. After the blaze, working-class families were pushed out in favor of industrial development. *Top:* This photo from 1907 shows Third Street from Howard to Market as workers rebuilt what had been lost. *Bottom:* That same intersection is pictured today, where one can find the San Francisco Museum of Modern Art and adjacent Yerba Buena Gardens.

Shot Tower

As South of Market grew more industrialized after 1906, its population became increasingly male and transient. Boxing arenas thrived, apartment houses rose, and employment agencies and church missions swept in to help men who found themselves between jobs. In the 1930s, the Great Depression cast a shadow over the quarter, with Howard Street emerging as the local "skid row" (above, in 1937). According to *Collier's* magazine, it was "the dirtiest, drinkingest, and most depressing thoroughfare" in the entire city. Such conditions contributed to labor conflicts, especially the general strike in May 1934, which resulted in violence along the waterfront. Local unemployment plummeted during World War II, when shipyards boomed and slum-clearance projects later targeted the area. But ten percent of San Franciscans still live below the poverty level, and a head count in 2007 found more than 6,000 homeless people in this city.

Smokestacks were so profuse in the late 19th century that the South of Market skyline resembled a giant's pincushion. Factories poured pollutants into the air, putting the health of residents at risk. Then the San Francisco Gas Works coated the nearby waterfront with refuse coal tar—enough of it that the industrialized northeastern corner of this district came to be known as Tar Flat. Thomas H. Selby contributed much to the haze of contaminants that hung over the city. His North Beach ore-smelting works operated around the clock, but it was his "shot tower" at First and Howard streets (above, in the 1860s or '70s, and that same intersection today) that is best remembered. Made of brick and standing 200 feet tall, it was built in 1865 to produce ammunition from the pig lead put out by his smelter. Molten lead that was poured from the top of the tower broke into tiny spherical balls as it fell, and those balls were caught in a water-filled basin at the bottom. The shot tower was a tourist attraction for a good quarter of a century. Selby, who had arrived in the Bay Area from New York during the gold rush, was elected in 1869 as San Francisco's 13th mayor and went on to build a stately "country home" for himself and his society-loving wife on Rincon Hill.

HERB CAEN GOT HIS WAY

Herb Caen

IN 1996, THE HISTORIC 3.2-mile promenade alongside the Embarcadero—from Fisherman's Wharf down to what's now AT&T Park—was christened Herb Caen Way… in honor of the Pulitzer Prize–winning newspaper columnist who dubbed San Francisco "Baghdad-by-the-Bay," referring to its multiculturalism. The Sacramento-born, martini-swilling Caen began writing for the *San Francisco Chronicle* in 1938, worked for most of the 1950s at the rival *Examiner,* and finished out his life with the *Chronicle* again. He died at age 80 in 1997. Caen was known for his unabashed love of San Francisco as much as he was known for the six columns a week he churned out over most of six decades, each peppered with three-dot item dividers (like the signs along Herb Caen Way…). During the festivities surrounding the opening of his promenade, Caen said, "When it's my time, if I get to heaven, I'm going to say what every San Franciscan says when they get to heaven: 'It ain't bad, but it ain't San Francisco.'"

Strike Town

Local labor relations came to a violent head during the summer of 1934. Dockworkers in San Francisco, as well as at other ports along the West Coast, went on strike *(above)* on May 9 to win union representation, a union-run hiring hall, and a coast-wide contract. They were joined days later by sailors.

Employers responded by hiring strikebreakers, and battles between dockworkers and their temporary replacements erupted all over the coast. The largest confrontation took place in San Francisco on July 5, when some thousand police officers were called in to clear picketers from the waterfront and allow strikebreakers to work. On that afternoon, known infamously as "Bloody Thursday," two picketers were killed and more than 60 others were injured. When police refused to back down and California's governor, Frank Merriam, called on the National Guard to keep peace along the waterfront, dozens of Bay Area unions endorsed a four-day general strike in protest against the police violence.

Tensions remained high until an arbitration proposal was approved by workers in late July. That settlement brought Pacific Coast longshore workers increased wages, enhanced bargaining rights, and strength in the hiring process—most of what they'd wanted in the first place.

Crystal Palace Market

Talk to someone who grew up here in the 1930s or '40s, and he or she is likely to have fond memories of the Crystal Palace Market at Eighth and Market streets (shown here in the 1950s). Erected during Prohibition, it was a colorful, European-style shopping mall with stands from which vendors sold meat, vegetables, cheeses, cigars, house pets, and honey. You could order sandwiches and eat them while sitting on round stools and chatting with friends. Or you could drop by the Anchor Brewing Company for a glass of steam beer. While parents bought groceries, their children would wander the packed aisles, stopping for samples of peanut butter (the proprietor let them dip wooden spoons into his huge vats out front), invest their few coins in ice cream, or watch as a man peddling soaps wound live snakes around his wrists and neck. The Crystal Palace finally closed its doors in 1959, unable to compete with more modern stores.

San Francisco Mint

San Francisco has had a U.S. Mint ever since the mid-1850s, when one opened on Commercial Street to serve the California gold mines. However, that original plant was overwhelmed by silver gushing out of Nevada's Comstock Lode and had to be replaced in 1874 by this granite Greek Revival edifice at Fifth and Mission streets (below, in 1875). It was the work of British-born designer Alfred B. Mullett. The Mint was one of only two major public buildings in the South of Market district to survive the 1906 disaster (the other was the U.S. Court of Appeals Building at Seventh and Mission streets). In 1937, the "Old Mint," as it's now called, was replaced by a newer facility in Hayes Valley. Mullett's structure is now a National Historic Landmark and slated to become home to the Museum of San Francisco and the Bay Area (right). Above: The Old Mint's Coin Room in the late 1800s, where stacks of newly minted currency were counted and packaged.

RINCON HILL

Rising 100 feet above Market Street to the south and offering excellent views across Yerba Buena Cove, Rincon Hill welcomed considerable upscale residential construction during the 1850s. Its early dwellers included newspaper owner and civic promoter Samuel Brannan, banker and future Civil War commander William Tecumsah Sherman, hotelier and later amusement park owner Robert B. Woodward, and cable-car entrepreneur Andrew S. Hallidie. Both the wealthy and the wannabes congregated in this quarter, erecting stately abodes in a wide range of architectural styles. From Gothic to Second Empire, many of these houses were accessorized with sumptuous gardens and elegant carriages. This photograph is looking north from Rincon Hill toward congested Yerba Buena Cove in the 1860s or '70s. The octagonal home in the lower right was apparently once occupied by Margaret Wyman, author Bret Harte's sister. Not long ago, Rincon Hill began transitioning into a more densely packed residential area *(top right)*. This mount is also the touch-down point for the Bay Bridge.

Milton S. Latham Home

Shown in the early 1870s *(right)*, this was the home of Milton S. Latham, an Ohio-born attorney who moved to San Francisco in 1850 and soon after entered politics. Nine years later, Latham was elected the Democratic governor of California—only to resign a record five days into his term to become the state's junior U.S. senator. He replaced David C. Broderick, who had recently been killed in a pistol duel with former state Supreme Court Justice David S. Terry. By the time this photograph was taken, Rincon Hill was already in decline. Industrial development along its southern flank and completion of the "Second Street Cut" destroyed Rincon Hill's standing with the city's elite. As cable-car lines eased transportation up the heights of Nob Hill (more than three times taller than Rincon), many members of this neighborhood's upper crust migrated north to that less-built-up prominence.

SOUTH PARK

Located between Bryant and Brannan streets from Second to Third, the once fashionable enclave of South Park was the brainchild of George Gordon, the scion of a well-to-do family from Yorkshire, England. After marrying a barmaid in a drunken spree, a mortified Gordon set sail with his new spouse for California, determined to start a fresh life. He accumulated huge profits from sugar refining and an iron foundry, and he began purchasing lots on the southwest slope of Rincon Hill in the early 1850s. In collaboration with English-born architect and artist George H. Goddard, Gordon built an oval, gated park that was 75 feet wide and 550 feet long (above, in the 1860s or '70s). It was surrounded by uniform, two-story Italianate row houses that he sold to financiers and other mandarins put off by the "cold and uninhabitable" western reaches of town. Unfortunately for Gordon, the 1855 California banking collapse doomed his dream of a residential community similar to Berkeley Square. He died 14 years later, but not before seeing his beloved daughter, Nellie, turned into an alcoholic by his habitually intoxicated wife and then wed a doctor against her father's wishes—a tragedy fictionalized by San Francisco author Gertrude Atherton in *A Daughter of the Vine* (1899).

In 1869, the year George Gordon passed away, the infamous "Second Street Cut" slashed through Rincon Hill, passing just east of South Park and connecting downtown to the city's southern waterfront. Once isolated, South Park was suddenly trafficked by blue-collar workers and the laboring poor, whose new residency in the area ruined its former prestige. In 1897, Gordon's private park was acquired by the city, which took off the locks and opened it to the public. During the 1906 catastrophe, most of this district was fried and flattened, but the oval commons was later restored. And in the 1990s, South Park became fashionable all over again, this time as the center of San Francisco's short-lived dot-com boom. Businesses there are more diverse now, but the neighborhood has regained some acclaim as an urban oasis.

South Beach

Like so many of the coves and bays that once gave jagged shape to San Francisco's waterfront, South Beach—located north of China Basin and south of what used to be Rincon Point, near where the Bay Bridge bounds toward Oakland—has been filled and flattened so that little remains of its natural topography. Where condominium developments now crowd together and furniture shoppers break their pace to sip wines or tequilas, there used to be low sand cliffs and a sloping half-moon of shoreline from which boats were easily launched. By the late 19th century, though, lots owned by fishers were being bought by industrialists determined to make the city a shipping and shipbuilding capital. The photo here, shot in the mid-1860s, shows St. Mary's Hospital on the left. Built in 1857 at First and Bryant streets, it had to be abandoned in the onslaught of fire in 1906, and its patients were loaded onto a ferry and shipped to Oakland. The large building on the right is the Sailors' Relief Home.

SAN FRANCISCO BASEBALL

Baseball has been played in San Francisco ever since the gold rush, when one of the sport's originators, New York City bookseller Alexander Cartwright, arrived in California hoping to get rich. Although health concerns soon drove him to Hawaii, he left behind what would become the "national pastime." In 1903, a team dubbed the San Francisco Seals became a charter member of the Pacific Coast League (PCL). Games were played in South of Market's Recreation Park at Eighth and Harrison streets until that field was destroyed in 1906. A new Recreation Park soon went up at 14th and Valencia in the Mission District. In 1926, the city acquired a second minor-league baseball franchise: the San Francisco Mission Reds (or "Missions," as they were known). Transplants from Los Angeles, they played at Recreation Park when the Seals were on the road. Five years later, the Seals and Missions both relocated to a new ballpark at 16th and Bryant streets in Potrero Hill.

A 17-year-old North Beach boy named Joe DiMaggio signed with the Seals at the end of the 1932 season, and a year later he hit safely in 61 games—a professional baseball record. Francis "Lefty" O'Doul, a former major-leaguer who had returned to his native San Francisco as the Seals' manager, led the team to its last pennant of the decade in 1935. The Missions transferred to Los Angeles in 1938 and became the Hollywood Stars. DiMaggio went on to a Hall of Fame career with the New York Yankees. O'Doul, though, stayed with the Seals until 1951 and then founded a namesake restaurant in the Union Square area. Finally, the team moved to Arizona for the 1958 season, making room for the New York Giants, who came to California along with the Brooklyn Dodgers.

Above: The 15,000-seat Recreation Park, located in the Mission District, was the home of the San Francisco Seals of the Pacific Coast League from 1907 to 1930.
Left: Electrifying outfielder Willie Mays, who many claim is the greatest player in National League history, belted 459 home runs and won 11 Gold Gloves in his 14-plus years in San Francisco.

AT&T Park

In 1960, the San Francisco Giants began four decades of play at Candlestick Park in the city's windy, foggy southeast corner. During that time, the team fielded some powerhouse players including Willie Mays, Gaylord Perry, and Joe Montefusco. The team won three National League pennants (most recently in 1989, when their World Series contest with the Oakland A's was interrupted by the Loma Prieta earthquake). The team also courted controversy in 2007, when Barry Bonds hit his 756th home run, beating slugger Hank Aaron's 33-year-old record and reigniting debate over Bonds's alleged steroid use. Fans who had shivered through games at "The Stick" cheered when the Giants moved to a $319 million stadium on the South Beach waterfront in 2000. Like the old Recreation Park, this new facility, AT&T Park (formerly called Pacific Bell Park), is notorious for home runs hit out of the arena—only now those fly balls land in the Bay rather than in city streets. They're called "splash hits."

BAY BRIDGE

Although there was some opposition to building the Golden Gate Bridge, mostly from people who feared it would damage the channel's scenic views, the proposed San Francisco-Oakland Bay Bridge (or Bay Bridge, as it's come to be called) prompted little resistance. The federal government even fronted the project $77 million with coaxing by President Herbert Hoover, a Stanford graduate. This is something the government had not done for its sister span to the west, which was financed through the sale of bonds to public and private investors. For the Bay Bridge, the more important issue was one of engineering. It was expected to cross about four and a half miles of water—quadruple the distance covered by the Golden Gate Bridge. Chief engineer Charles H. Purcell, assisted by a board of consultants including renowned Polish-born bridge designer Ralph Modjeski, resolved to construct *two* bridges, not just one. The first was a two-mile-long suspension span stretching from Rincon Hill to tiny Yerba Buena Island. There, the roadway would enter a 1,700-foot-long tunnel, the excavation of which would provide debris to be used in creating adjacent Treasure Island. The rest of the crossing, from the island east to Oakland, would be made by a traditional cantilever bridge. *Top:* The bridge under construction in 1935.

The Bay Bridge welcomed traffic for the first time in November 1936. More than two dozen lives were lost during its construction, and it cost a whopping $77 million. But building this bridge created thousands of jobs during the crushing Depression, and it helped open San Francisco to more convenient travel beyond its borders.

Left: In February 1937, a woman helps dedicate the new sign telling motorists where the Bay Bridge crosses San Francisco's city limit into Oakland.

The Bay Bridge now carries more than 280,000 vehicles a day, most of them occupied by commuters. That's a heavy load, and one that engineers say its eastern, cantilevered component cannot bear for much longer. The 7.1-magnitude Loma Prieta earthquake in October 1989 did significant damage to the eastern half of this bridge, collapsing part of its upper deck onto the lower one. While the bridge was shut down for a month for repairs, seismic experts determined that while its western portion could be retrofitted to withstand a major quake in the future, it would be more cost-effective to replace the cantilevered-truss eastern span. That replacement, a more elegant suspension bridge, is expected to open for business by 2010.

GOLDEN GATE INTERNATIONAL EXPOSITION

Not only were designers of the Golden Gate International Exposition working their magic on a brand-new island in the Bay, but they were aiming to create a new style of architecture as well. They strived for one that blended modernism's functionality with designs from all around the Pacific Basin. Particularly evident were Mayan and Asian influences. Exhibit halls stood a uniform 100 feet tall and were windowless, which contributed to their air of monumentality. The main fairgrounds took the shape of a huge cross, its center occupied by the Tower of the Sun, a 392-foot, sleekly updated cousin of the 1915 fair's Tower of Jewels. Created by Arthur Brown, Jr., who had previously designed City Hall and Coit Tower, this spire quickly became the 1939 fair's familiar symbol, featured on posters and postcards.

Above: Brown's tower was fronted on the west by artist and architect Donald Macky's pyramidal (and controversial) Elephant Towers. Their look was inspired by the historic temples of Southeast Asia and Central America, and their name was spawned by the stylized elephants and the howdahs (the seat and canopy on top of the elephant) that formed their peaks.

Treasure Island's main administrative building is one of the few structures remaining from the Expo. Statues erected for the fair still flank the entrance.

Sally Rand's Nude Ranch

Although the Golden Gate Exposition claimed serious intent, it also provided entertainment like other world's fairs. Musicians such as Benny Goodman and Count Basie arrived to play the most popular music of the day, swing. Burlesque dancer and actress Sally Rand, whose suggestive "bubble dance" had shocked many spectators during Chicago's 1933 Century of Progress fair, brought to San Francisco an even more outlandish attraction: Sally Rand's Nude Ranch. The moniker said it all. On a miniature dude ranch, young women demonstrated their roping and riding capabilities, all while wearing hats, boots, and not much else.

POTRERO HILL

The Potrero Hill neighborhood is bordered roughly by 16th and Cesar Chavez streets to the north and south, Potrero Avenue on the west, and the waterfront on the east. The area's history dates to the 1830s and a land grant made to rancher Francisco de Haro. He served as the first *alcalde* (mayor) of minuscule Yerba Buena during its Mexican period and grazed cattle from Mission Dolores on his *potrero nuevo* (new pasture). Eventually, cows were driven away to make room for gold rush squatters, and then successive waves of immigrants: Scots, Irish, Chinese, Russians, Mexicans, and in the 1940s, African Americans from the South, who came here looking for shipyard work during World War II. The district was known for its dense industrialization from the late 19th century through the 20th century. But residents found in this neighborhood a quiet, surprisingly fog-free escape from busy downtown San Francisco. Both photographs show 24th Street and Potrero Avenue, above in 1929, and right today.

Potrero Point, a once steep-banked ridge that formed the southern edge of Mission Bay, was exploited by early capitalists for its deepwater access. Boat builders began operating there shortly after the gold rush, but it wasn't until 1883 that it became home to the Union Iron Works (UIW), an iron-casting foundry that had operated in the South of Market district before moving heavily into the shipbuilding trade (shown above, circa late 1800s). In 1885, the UIW launched the first steel-hulled ship built on the Pacific Rim and constructed 75 marine vessels over the next 18 years. These included Commodore George Dewey's U.S. Navy flagship, the USS *Olympia,* and the battleship *Oregon,* both of which saw action in the Philippines during the Spanish-American War. In 1906, Massachusetts-based Bethlehem Steel purchased the shipyard. During World Wars I and II, more than 150 vessels were built there, many of them combat craft. Later, the steel tubes that carry BART trains under the Bay were constructed at the Potrero yards. The Port of San Francisco now owns the property but leases it to a large-scale ship-repair operation.

IRISH HILL

AT ONE TIME, POTRERO HILL was more divided along trade and ethnic lines than it is today. Butchertown, full of slaughterhouses that reeked of rotting meat and leaked blood into street gutters, extended northeast from Seals Stadium to 3rd Street. Russian immigrants began arriving there in the early 1900s and settled on the hill's western flank, which naturally became known as Little Russia. Irish Hill (shown above in the 1890s with the Union Iron Works in the background) rose up just west of the waterfront, its rocky heights packed with cottages, boardinghouses, and hotels. While proper San Francisco boasted of operas and vaudeville theaters, Irish Hill often found its entertainment in good-natured fistfights. Gang warfare over worker pay and the saloon trade contributed to Irish Hill's roughneck image. By the end of World War I, most of Irish Hill had been blasted away and the rock used as bayside landfill.

The Winning of the West

This city's oldest intact building is La Misión de San Francisco de Asís, better known today as Mission Dolores. The area was chosen by Captain Juan Bautista de Anza and Franciscan brother Pedro Font, who came in 1776 to site a new mission and presidio on the peninsula. That same year, Father Francisco Palóu—a disciple of Father Junípero Serra, who initiated California's 21 Spanish Catholic missions—dedicated this settlement to St. Francis of Assisi, who founded the Franciscan Order in the 13th century.

The original chapel and mission are said to have stood on what's now Camp Street. Construction of the present Mission Dolores at Dolores Street and 16th Avenue began in 1785. At its peak in the early 19th century, this church was the nexus of a community—far removed from the developing town of Yerba Buena—that included farms, ranches, health-care services, and facilities for manufacturing wool cloth and other products. It was also located not far from navigable Mission Creek, which extended west from Mission Bay, a large, marshy cove since filled in and covered with parts of the Potrero Hill and South of Market neighborhoods.

By the early 1850s, a plank-covered toll road (the beginning of modern-day Mission Street) was bringing cargo wagons, carriage-riding sightseers, and prospective inhabitants to the Mission District.

A streetcar line finally reached the Mission in 1866, and the quarter became popular with well-to-do families who appreciated its semirural attributes and the fact that fog burned off earlier in the day here than in other sectors of the city.

NEW DISCOVERIES

Transportation advances, coupled with the availability of huge tracts of land that had previously been held by a few old families, invited commercial and residential development of this and San Francisco's other western territories. Much of the acreage to the west of Civic Center had, until the late 19th century, harbored only small, autonomous villages and a profusion of squatters. Disputes between the civic and federal governments over which one had the best claim to some of the so-called Outside Lands slowed the city's spread. However, as more people moved into San

A gay couple strolls through the Castro District, or simply "the Castro," dubbed the country's gay and lesbian capital.

Left: Students protest segregation on Fillmore Street in May 1963.

A young Haight-Ashbury local poses in 1968 with a member of the older set, who sold newspapers to pay for food.

Francisco, they looked for new vicinities in which to stake claims. Places such as Noe Valley, the Western Addition, and the Mission started rumbling with the sounds of construction.

A DIVERSE CROWD

So did Eureka Valley. If you can't find that on a map, it's because most people know it today as the Castro District. Named for General José Castro, descended from a member of de Anza's exploring party, this area west of the Mission got started in the late 1880s, when a cable railway reached here from downtown. By the early 20th century, it had been dubbed "Little Scandinavia" for its heavy immigrant concentration of Swedes, Finns, and Norwegians. Next came the Irish, turning the Castro into a working-class enclave. And beginning in the late '60s, it came to be identified as the gay and lesbian capital of America, its sidewalk parades enriched by transvestites in stiletto heels and men with colored scarves dangling from their jeans pockets to announce their sexual preferences. (The scarf is apparently a tradition from the gold-rush era, when there were so few women in these parts that men had to dance with each other, and they indicated their preference for leading or following by the hue of their bandannas.) More recently, gay and lesbian couples have been leaving for cheaper urban locales or homes outside the city. Yet the Castro's rep as a "gayborhood" still draws gay and lesbian visitors from around the world.

Demographic change is familiar throughout this diverse division of town.

The Mission District, for instance, was once rife with workers from Germany, Poland, and Ireland. By the mid-20th century, whites were raising for-sale signs on their lawns and Hispanic families were moving in. Today, many people view the Mission, with its Latino murals, annual carnaval festival, and architectural odes to Spanish abodes, as a survivor from San Francisco's 19th-century Mexican era. However, its history isn't anywhere near as consistent. The same can be said of the Fillmore District (named for the 13th U.S. president, Millard Fillmore), which started out as a heavily Jewish quarter but gained fame as the center of the local African American jazz scene after World War II.

LOVING "THE HAIGHT"

The area with perhaps the quickest swing of population was the Haight-Ashbury. Originally a wealthy resort community adjacent to Golden Gate Park, it turned into a haven for hippies, heirs to the Beats' sense of societal alienation, in the 1960s. These young rebels came to experiment with drugs, hang out with the likes of Janis Joplin and the Grateful Dead (who had a house—still standing—at 710 Ashbury), and find a bit of false utopia. "The Haight-Ashbury district of San Francisco is not so much a neighborhood as a state of mindlessness," *Time* quipped in 1967. Within just a couple of years, though, the Haight's "turn on, tune in, drop out" days were done, and it was well on its way to being home to those upper-middle-class professionals the nonconforming hippies swore they would never become. But soon did.

MISSION DOLORES

The Mission Dolores we know today was built, beginning in 1785, by Native American Christian converts and was dedicated on August 2, 1791. Its four-foot-thick walls were constructed of more than 36,000 adobe bricks, and redwood beams and trusses—originally lashed together with rawhide—were put up to support a roof covered with clay tiles. Punctuating the church's white, multicolumned facade are three niches holding bells brought from Mexico in the 1820s. During the early 19th century, a two-story wooden wing, meant to hold a seminary and priests' quarters, was tacked onto the church's north side. In honor of San Francisco's centennial in 1876, and to accommodate the city's growing population (without having to make severe changes to the old adobe structure), a Gothic Revival brick parish church was raised on the north side of the mission. However, the parish's structural integrity was severely compromised by the 1906 quake, and it was subsequently demolished. The photo above shows the mission in the 1860s or '70s.

Mission Dolores's interior displays an intersection of old California cultures. The baroque-style relief sculpture that backdrops the main altar is called a *reredos,* and it was hand-carved in Mexico and shipped north in pieces in 1796. It conceals behind it a less ostentatious religious mural, created on the chapel's back wall a few years earlier by Native Americans who were living at the Mission. The ceiling and beams are decorated in a zigzag motif that resembles local Indian basket designs and imitates colors originally applied with vegetable dyes. Holy water fonts at the chapel's rear are made from Chinese plates brought to California from the Philippines aboard 18th-century Spanish galleons. It's astonishing how little the church's interior has changed since this photo was taken in 1909.

In 1913, construction began on a brand-new parish church beside Mission Dolores. Although built in the California Mission style, it was constructed of concrete and steel to protect it against future earthquakes. The designers were Frank T. Shea, an École des Beaux-Arts alumnus, and his partner, John O. Lofquist. The church was dedicated on Christmas Day 1918. During the 1920s, Henry Minton, another San Francisco architect, undertook an extensive redecoration of the church's facade, adding the Spanish Baroque embellishments. In 1952, Pope Pius XII elevated Mission Dolores to the status of a minor basilica—the first one west of the Mississippi River.

Mission Dolores Cemetery

From the time of Mission Dolores's founding until 1898, burials took place in and around the church. Inside are still found the remains of several notables, such as José Joaquin Moraga, the Spanish military commander who led the first colonizing party to San Francisco in 1776; William Leidesdorff, who in the 1840s made his fortune in these parts as a businessman and his name as a politician; and the Reverend Richard Carroll, who served as Mission Dolores's first pastor after San Francisco became an archdiocese in the 1850s. The surrounding grounds once harbored thousands of graves. (The photo shows the cemetery in the 1860s.) There is also a monument to some 5,000 Christianized Indians who were interred in unmarked plots outside of today's pleasant, leafy funerary ground. A scene from Alfred Hitchcock's 1958 movie thriller, *Vertigo,* found Kim Novak and Jimmy Stewart visiting this graveyard.

DOLORES PARK

Located just south of Mission Dolores on the border between the Mission and Castro districts is the almost 14-acre greensward known as Dolores Park. Most visitors to this oasis probably don't know that the site was once occupied by not one, but *two* cemeteries. The property was purchased in the early 1860s by members of San Francisco's two Jewish congregations for use as a final resting place. (This photo shows the burial ground at 18th and Dolores streets in 1876.) However, both graveyards were closed to further interments in the late 1880s or early '90s, when the property became too valuable to be occupied solely by the dead. Remains were soon removed to the necropolis-dominated town of Colma in San Mateo County. In 1905, the City of San Francisco bought the land and established Dolores Park, and a year later, 1,600 Mission District families sought refuge there after the great earthquake toppled homes and kicked up fires that threatened their historic neighborhood.

Dolores Park—officially Mission Dolores Park—has become this neighborhood's foremost gathering spot. Postcardlike views of downtown are available from this commons' northern end, and there too can be found Mission High School. It was founded in 1896 and is the oldest high school still on its original site in the city. Sunbathers and picnickers favor Dolores Park's south end. At the southwest corner, where 20th and Church streets intersect, sits a famous fire hydrant. During the 1906 disaster, when most water mains in the city were broken and fireplugs had gone dry, this humble hydrant continued to gush. It's now credited with saving much of the Mission District. Every April 18—the anniversary of the great earthquake and fire—volunteers ceremoniously give this old plug a fresh coat of gold paint in remembrance.

Mission Street in December 1949, when it won the city's District Christmas Decorations Contest.

MISSION DISTRICT

Mission Street, from 16th Street south to César Chávez (formerly Army Street), may look a tad rough these days, but it boomed during the first half of the 20th century, when this neighborhood was a melting pot of working-class Irish, Italian, German, and Scandinavian families. During the late 1940s, when the retail corridor bustled with clothing shops, movie theaters, auto dealerships, and furniture outlets, local merchants banded together to rededicate it as the "Mission Miracle Mile." They mounted Mexican-style archways over the avenue and imitation bell towers at street corners, staged contests to choose pretty Miracle Mile Maids, and at Christmastime decorated the road with wreaths and mission bells made from spun glass.

Mission Street today

ALEXANDER BERKMAN

Alexander Berkman was born in Lithuania but became infamous in the United States. An ardent anarchist and lover of political activist Emma Goldman, the then 22-year-old Berkman tried in 1892 to murder industrialist Henry Clay Frick in Pittsburgh, in revenge for the deaths of steelworkers who had perished during Frick's put-down of a labor dispute. Frick survived, and Berkman was imprisoned for 14 years. After his release, the rabble-rouser wrote for Goldman's radical political periodical, *Mother Earth,* and led anticapitalist protests in New York that resulted in an attempted bombing of oil mogul John D. Rockefeller's country home in 1914. From 1916 to 1917, Berkman lived in San Francisco, where he started an anarchist magazine called *The Blast*. It lasted only 29 issues, until he was arrested for inciting resistance to the World War I draft. During his time here, Berkman occupied one of half a dozen flats in a still-standing building at 569 Dolores Street *(above),* adjacent to Dolores Park. He was later deported to the Soviet Union, and he committed suicide in 1936.

WOODWARD'S GARDENS

Woodward's Gardens was not San Francisco's first public playground, but it stood quite apart from its predecessors. Opened in 1866, it was the brainchild of Robert Woodward, a grocer turned hotelier (he was proprietor of the What Cheer House at Sacramento and Leidesdorff streets) who, as his wallet fattened, invested in Mission District real estate. In the late 1850s, he bought four acres of land bounded by what are today Mission and Valencia streets between 13th and 15th (property that had previously belonged to explorer-politician John C. Frémont). There, he constructed a substantial Victorian residence orbited by gardens, fountains, and aviaries. He even put together his own private art gallery. All of this attracted the curiosity of San Francisco's less well-to-do, and people started showing up at his estate, especially on Sundays, just to peer through the surrounding fence. When the crowds grew big enough, Woodward—bearing in his soul a little bit of Phineas T. Barnum, founder of the spectacle that became the Ringling Bros. and Barnum & Bailey Circus—moved his family out of town and re-created his estate as an amusement park. *Top:* The front gate at Mission and 14th streets, circa 1877.

On what was once hilly land, Woodward built a dance hall, a theater, flowered terraces, and a roller-skating rink. An arena hosted Roman chariot races, and the nation's first saltwater aquarium at the Gardens included a variety of colorful fish. Woodward offered the most complete zoo on the West Coast, with buffalo, zebras, and camels. Grizzly and black bears boasted their own pits, including platforms from which they could watch the crowds and be watched in return (left, circa 1877). Everywhere, the barking of sea lions could be heard, the scent of roasted popcorn followed, and ostriches wandering loose always looked ready to pounce on your picnic lunch.

Chang, "the Heathen Chinee Giant"

Human performers rivaled the draw of the Gardens' wildlife. Members of Walter Morosco's Royal Russian Circus thrilled audiences with their trapeze acts and acrobatic extravaganzas. Painted and befeathered Native Americans engaged in tribal dances. Fire-eaters from India provoked gasps among watchers. A Frenchman named Christal wrestled bears. Herman the Great regularly submitted to being blasted from a cannon. An amphitheater hosted Gilbert and Sullivan's *HMS Pinafore* and Yankee Robinson's *Ballet of Parisian Beauties*. And then, just when you were sure that this Mission park could offer no more surprises, around the corner would stroll the imposing figure of Chang, "the Heathen Chinee Giant," 8 feet, 3 inches tall in colorful silk robes and slowly flapping a paper fan (above, in the late 1800s).

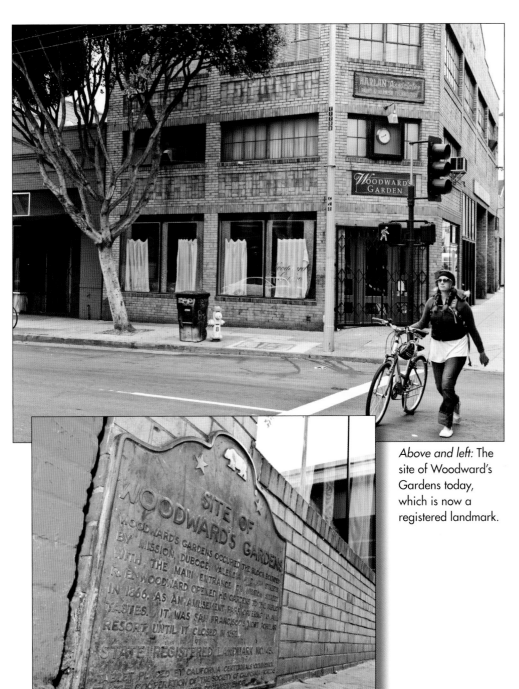

Above and left: The site of Woodward's Gardens today, which is now a registered landmark.

CASTRO DISTRICT

Borrowing from the architectural vernacular that inspired Henry Minton's exterior embellishments on the nearby Mission Dolores Basilica, San Francisco–born architect Timothy L. Pflueger gave his Castro Theatre similarly flamboyant Spanish Baroque exterior decoration, with its facade dominated by a great arched window. Opened in 1922 on Castro Street, near its intersection with Market and 17th streets, this movie palace was the first of several distinguished theaters Pflueger designed during a career that also found him creating South of Market's soaring art moderne Pacific Telephone Building (140 New Montgomery Street) and Oakland's massive art deco Paramount Theatre. In addition, Pflueger served as a lead architect for the 1939–40 Golden Gate International Exposition. The Castro Theatre (shown above in 1922 and at right in 2008) was designated a City of San Francisco landmark in 1977, and its neon sign has become a symbol for both the theater and its encircling neighborhood.

AMERICA'S GAYEST CITY

SAN FRANCISCO'S GAY and lesbian history may stretch back to the gold rush, when newspapers talked obliquely about "lavender cowboys" making rounds of Northern California's male-oriented camps. The gay population here rose significantly during World War II, when U.S. armed forces sought to identify and expel homosexual servicemen, many of whom were shipped back to the States through the Bay Area. A considerable number of those soldiers settled in more liberal San Francisco. North Beach contributed further to the emergence of the city's postwar gay community, as homosexual artists settled in the neighborhood. Following 1967's Summer of Love, the Castro became home base for the local gay and lesbian minority. Activists such as Harvey Milk—the self-proclaimed "Mayor of Castro Street" and the first openly gay member of the Board of Supervisors—were soon making significant inroads in local politics. The AIDS epidemic that began in the 1980s took a devastating toll on the Castro, but the area made a comeback during the dot-com boom of the '90s. The percentage of San Franciscans who identify themselves as gay, lesbian, or bisexual currently exceeds 15 percent, and among large American metropolises, this city has the highest concentration of same-sex households. Both figures may rise as a result of the California Supreme Court's 2008 decision to legalize same-sex marriage in the Bear State.

Left: San Francisco Supervisor Harvey Milk rides in the seventh annual Gay Freedom Parade on June 26, 1978. *Above:* With its rainbow flags waving, Castro Street today still has a bustling gay population.

HAIGHT-ASHBURY

The Haight-Ashbury, purportedly named in honor of two mid-19th century city supervisors, took a long time to bloom. Dominated by sand dunes lightly interspersed with farms (such as the one at right, photographed in 1892), this area remained largely undeveloped until 1883, when a cable railway shot through from Market Street to the main body of Golden Gate Park. Hotels and saloons quickly sprang up around the cable-car turnaround at Haight and Stanyan streets to service both weekend visitors to the park and the affluent San Franciscans who were building "country homes" nearby. Yet it wasn't until the early 1900s that developers got busy grading and subdividing the acreage east of the park and south of the Panhandle in order to construct single-family residences, most of them gingerbread confections in the Queen Anne style. Contrary to its present image, the Haight was a solidly middle-class and rather conservative place a century ago, with a population made up of Germans, Scots, and Australians, as well as native-born Americans.

Like other areas west of downtown, this neighborhood escaped serious earthquake and fire injury in 1906, and many people later relocated to the Haight, thinking they'd be safer. The district was already short of open, available property by 1910, and by the start of World War I, what had been a leisure-time resort was transformed into an urban quarter with an active business district along Haight Street. However, the Great Depression of the 1930s was brutal on this neighborhood, as it was on other parts of San Francisco. Residents who could afford to move left for exclusive enclaves such as St. Francis Wood or Forest Hill, while many of the Haight's elegant Victorians were subdivided into low-rent and poorly maintained apartments to house wartime workers. The Haight-Ashbury slipped into a decades-long sleep. *Left:* Haight Street looking west from Ashbury, November 1944.

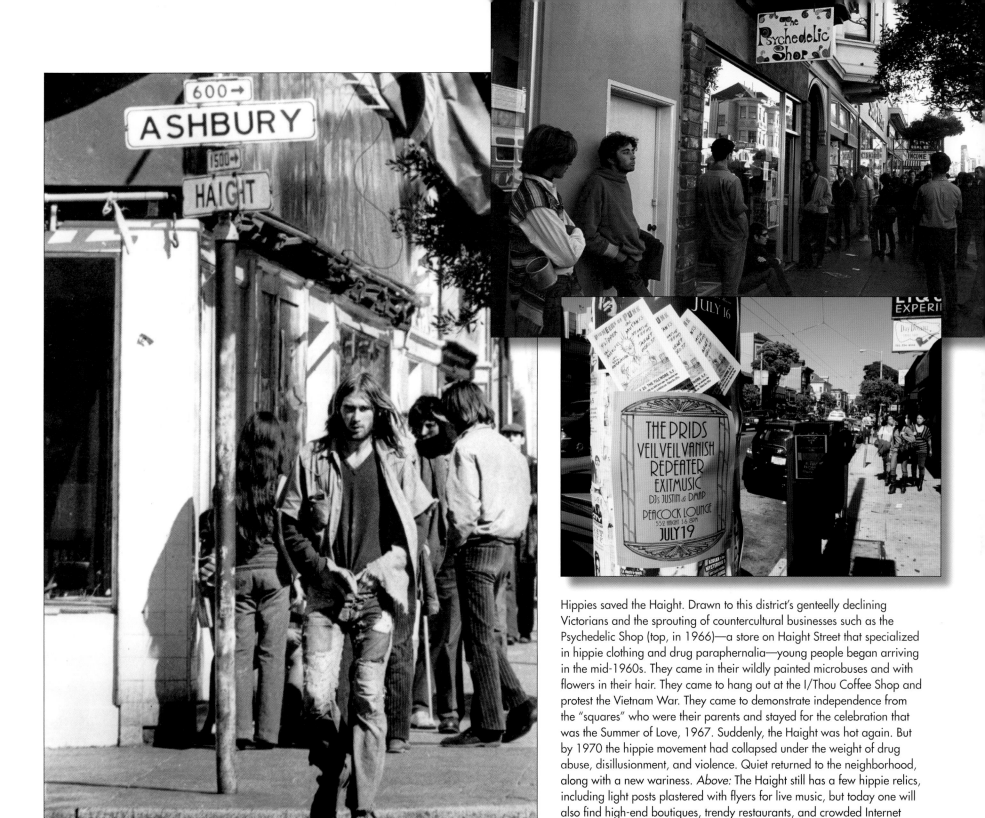

Hippies saved the Haight. Drawn to this district's genteelly declining Victorians and the sprouting of countercultural businesses such as the Psychedelic Shop (top, in 1966)—a store on Haight Street that specialized in hippie clothing and drug paraphernalia—young people began arriving in the mid-1960s. They came in their wildly painted microbuses and with flowers in their hair. They came to hang out at the I/Thou Coffee Shop and protest the Vietnam War. They came to demonstrate independence from the "squares" who were their parents and stayed for the celebration that was the Summer of Love, 1967. Suddenly, the Haight was hot again. But by 1970 the hippie movement had collapsed under the weight of drug abuse, disillusionment, and violence. Quiet returned to the neighborhood, along with a new wariness. *Above:* The Haight still has a few hippie relics, including light posts plastered with flyers for live music, but today one will also find high-end boutiques, trendy restaurants, and crowded Internet cafés. *Left:* The corner of Haight and Ashbury in the 1960s.

WESTERN ADDITION

By the 1870s, streetcars were trundling out to the Western Addition, carrying folks who wished to pay their Sunday respects and picnic at the cemeteries around sandy Lone Mountain, the site of today's University of San Francisco campus. Convenient transportation also threw this district open to "suburban" residential construction. Before long, middle-class Victorian row houses were spreading, giving the neighborhood an air of architectural gentility that for many nonresidents still symbolizes San Francisco. Though developers sought to make the most of this new area, the city was more generous here in establishing public parks than it had been closer to downtown. Among those new parks was Alamo Square, on Steiner Street between Fulton and Hayes, which was graded and planted in the 1890s.
Above: A visitor to Alamo Square gazes west toward the high-domed, pre-earthquake City Hall, circa 1900.

By the 1940s, the Western Addition was suffering from serious overcrowding, the result in part of so many African Americans coming west for wartime employment. City planners looked around at the rickety wooden buildings and decided that this district needed to be flattened to be fixed. In the late 1950s, under the direction of M. Justin Herman, head of the San Francisco Redevelopment Agency (SFRA), the city began bulldozing large swaths of the Western Addition to replace Victorian homes with modern apartment blocks. But adequate consideration wasn't given to the needs of displaced low-income inhabitants, many of whom were unable to find accommodations elsewhere in town and were not financially able to move back once the neighborhood renewal was complete. In 1968, following riots and a torrent of lawsuits, a federal judge cut off funding for the redevelopment and halted the removal of residents. In the aftermath of that demolition was born the local preservation movement, and what had not been lost was rediscovered.

Alamo Square

Of the tens of thousands of polychromatic Victorian residences ("painted ladies") that were raised in San Francisco between the gold rush and the outbreak of World War I, the most photographed might be those half-dozen that line the 700 block of Steiner Street, on Alamo Square's western edge. They were constructed between 1892 and 1896 by local developer Matthew Kavanaugh, who reserved 722 Steiner for his own family.

THE MISTRESS OF MYSTERY

ABOLITIONIST, business-woman, and "voodoo queen," Mary Ellen Pleasant played a role in San Francisco history that seems both complex and contradictory. It's been said that "Mammy" Pleasant abducted indentured African Americans from the South and sent them via the Underground

The Old Pleasant/Bell Home at 1661 Octavia Street in 1925

Railroad to Ohio and Canada, where they could find freedom. It's been said, too, that she was at least half black but for decades passed as white, and under that pretext she reached the Bay Area in the early 1850s. Legend has it her first job here was as a cook for wealthy men, but within a few years she'd made enough from investments to acquire real estate and laundries; that she maintained tight control over the black community with spells and potions; and was responsible for several murders in her "House of Mystery."

What of that is true and what is slander propagated by her many enemies is hard to tell anymore. It is known that Pleasant prospered in San Francisco, that she helped fund abolitionist John Brown's 1859 raid on the federal arsenal at Harpers Ferry, Virginia, and that in the 1860s she led a campaign to desegregate this city's streetcars. According to the *San Francisco Chronicle*, her lawsuit against the streetcar companies "set a precedent in the California Supreme Court and was used in future civil rights cases, such as an 1893 case over segregation in housing."

It's for that last effort that she's best remembered. After Pleasant died in 1904, a marker was placed over her grave in Napa reading, "Mother of Civil Rights in California."

JAPANTOWN

Japanese immigrants established ethnic enclaves in Chinatown and South of Market during the late 19th century. But both were decimated by the 1906 earthquake and fire, and most of their residents moved to the Western Addition, creating a Japantown ("Nihonmachi") bordered roughly by O'Farrell, Pine, Fillmore, and Octavia streets. Even there, though, the Japanese could not find peace. Sometimes violent protests against their participation in the workforce, coupled with a local school-board effort to segregate their children, led the U.S. government in 1908 to restrict further immigration from Japan. In 1910, San Francisco claimed 4,700 Japanese residents. Thirty years later that number had climbed to just 5,280. The Japanese attack on Pearl Harbor, Hawaii, in 1941 cast suspicion upon all Japanese nationals and Japanese Americans on the West Coast. By government order, some 120,000 Japanese Americans were forced to sell or abandon their property and were sent to internment camps in the country's interior.

In April 1942, 664 San Franciscans of Japanese descent—the initial wave of evacuees—lined up with their bags on Van Ness Avenue to be bused out of town. The majority were incarcerated at the Topaz camp near Delta, Utah, where the population exceeded 8,000. They waited behind barbed wire until their release in 1945. Many who returned to Japantown found their homes occupied by African Americans who had moved here from the South in search of wartime industrial employment.

Miss Lake's School for Young Ladies

Opened in 1890 and designed by local architect Henry Schulze, who also did work on the Stanford University campus, this gracious Victorian structure on the corner of Sutter and Octavia streets was originally Miss Lake's School for Young Ladies (left, in 1890). Its construction was financed by Comstock "Silver King" and erstwhile U.S. Senator James G. Fair, reportedly in order to give his two daughters proper "finishing" in the feminine arts. (The fact that both girls grew up to marry wealthy men, one a Vanderbilt, might suggest that his investment was a good one.) But the school is believed to have closed after only a few years, leaving the edifice to become, at various times, a polished gentlemen's club and a residence for young working women. It's now an antiques-filled bed-and-breakfast known as the Queen Anne Hotel. Rumor has it that the place is haunted by the kindly ghost of former schoolmistress Mary Lake.

Peace Pagoda

Similar to the Western Addition, Japantown was hard hit by this city's mid-20th century redevelopment schemes. Many Victorian homes in this smallest of San Francisco districts were demolished, though a few along Bush and Sutter streets managed to survive. What have been substituted are modern structures, some showing Asian lines or embellishments. Japan Center, a three-block-long retail, hotel, and cultural complex at the core of this neighborhood, reclines between Post Street and Geary Boulevard. Its principal landmark is the five-tiered Peace Pagoda (above, in the 1960s or '70s, and at left today), designed by Tokyo architect Yoshiro Taniguchi and donated to San Francisco in 1968 by its sister city, Osaka. Surrounding that tower is Peace Plaza, which really comes into its own during the annual Cherry Blossom Festival in April and the Nihonmachi Street Fair every August.

FILLMORE DISTRICT

Most folks think of the Fillmore District—or as habitués know it, "the Fillmore"—as part of the surrounding Western Addition. But it's set apart by both history and character. Bordered arguably by Fillmore Street on the west, Geary and Grove on the north and south, and Van Ness Avenue on the east, this was a generally rural suburb until the early 20th century, populated mainly by hard-working German-Austrian Jews who enjoyed the city's lack of anti-Semitism. In 1906, when the earth shook downtown San Francisco to pieces and fire burned it to a crisp, the Fillmore survived largely unscathed. Within weeks, businesses, government offices, newspapers, and theaters all set up shop here while their digs elsewhere were being rebuilt. The photo at right, shot about a month after the Great Quake, shows Fillmore as "the new Market Street," crowded with temporary signs and no longer serving its neighborhood alone.

In 1909, when this photo of young newspaper hawkers was taken in front of Abraham's Pharmacy at McAllister and Fillmore streets, the neighborhood was known for its variety of specialty shops. Their numbers had increased after 1906, when many Jewish families, driven from their South of Market homes, resettled in the Fillmore alongside Italian, French, Irish, and Japanese transplants. Kosher markets popped up, their windows profuse with baked goods, spit-roasting chickens, and fresh-made candies. There was a pocket-edition tamale and tortilla factory on Steiner Street. Sausages were for sale at Heineman & Stern on McAllister, the Wagon on Post Street peddled what were said to be the best hamburgers in town, and the most coveted, jumbo-size challah breads were produced by Langendorf's Bakery.

Local merchants naturally hoped to retain some of the commercial prosperity they enjoyed in the aftermath of the citywide disaster. To that end, they began advertising this district's attractions. In 1907, they added a bit of glamour by installing mammoth sweeping metal arches, freckled with electric lightbulbs and dangling ornate globes from their elevated centers, at 14 intersections along Fillmore Street. *Right:* Looking east along Eddy Street from Fillmore, June 1926.

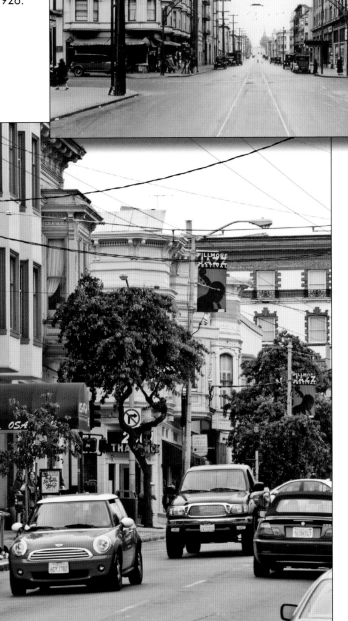

Fillmore Street today continues to be the neighorhood's main commercial strip, with diverse shops, markets, restaurants, and music venues.

Jimbo's Bop City

With America's entry into World War II, more than 400,000 African Americans moved west. In San Francisco, they sought employment with defense contractors and found relatively cheap housing in the Fillmore and Japantown areas. Before long, live-music venues were filling abandoned buildings all over this quarter, and by the 1950s, jazz, blues, and R&B could be heard at dozens of joints, including the New Orleans Swing Club, the Long Bar, and the Champagne Supper Club. They attracted artists on the order of Ella Fitzgerald, Louis Armstrong, Erroll Garner, Chet Baker, and Billie Holiday, plus celebrity fans such as Sammy Davis, Jr., and Clint Eastwood. The most legendary of those clubs may have been Jimbo's Bop City at Polk and Webster streets, which opened as a waffle shop but came to host such talents as saxophonists Norwood "Pony" Poindexter and Leo Wright (shown at right, playing Bop City in the '50s). Unfortunately, high postwar unemployment in the neighborhood and racial discrimination allowed the city to tear down blocks of homes and thereby destroy the clubs' economic base. By the 1970s, the Fillmore music scene was finished. The building that originally housed Bop City was moved to Fillmore Street and is now an African American bookstore.

Bill Graham

In 1912, the Majestic Hall and Majestic Academy of Music opened at Fillmore and Geary streets. An Italianate-style block designed by James and Merritt Reid, it hosted evening socials and masquerade balls. Over the next half century, the space was reborn as the Fillmore Auditorium and was used variously as a roller rink and a venue for big-name black musicians, including James Brown and Ike and Tina Turner. In the mid-1960s, a German-born promoter named Bill Graham (né Wolfgang Grajonca), shown at right in 1969, turned the hall into a world-renowned rock music theater. Graham booked most of the stars of early rock history, from local bands Jefferson Airplane, the Grateful Dead, and Creedence Clearwater Revival to Jimi Hendrix, Janis Joplin, and Pink Floyd. He also brought to the Fillmore non-rock acts such as Aretha Franklin and Otis Redding. In 1968, Graham moved his concerts to the old Carousel Ballroom, which he called Fillmore West, but he reopened the Fillmore in the 1980s.

In addition to being known for its music, the Fillmore Auditorium was recognized for the design of its psychedelic posters. Created by graphic artists such as Wes Wilson, Lee Conklin, Victor Moscoso, and Alton Kelly, those concert placards displayed the influences of art nouveau and Dadaism. They were richly colored, often symmetrically composed, and immediately recognizable for their ornate, fluid lettering—suggesting the mind-distorting influences of drugs. That style became synonymous with the 1960s and early '70s, and it was picked up by designers of record album covers. *Right:* The September 1966 appearances of Jefferson Airplane and others were promoted in this poster by Wilson, probably the most prolific of the Fillmore's artists.

Fillmore Auditorium

The Fillmore was damaged during the 1989 Loma Prieta earthquake, and Bill Graham died two years later in a helicopter crash. After being retrofitted, the auditorium opened once more in 1994 and continues to host concerts to this day. It has also become a tourist draw, especially when coupled with the space right next door on Geary, which once held a Scottish Rite Masonic temple. In 1971, that structure was occupied by the infamous Peoples Temple, a religious cult led by the Reverend Jim Jones. They aided the poor and homeless and curried favor with California politicians. Seven years later, Jones convinced his followers to abandon San Francisco and join him at an ostensibly utopian settlement in South America, later ordering them to drink cyanide-laced fruit drinks. More than 900 people died, and Jones perished from a gunshot wound. Their Peoples Temple in the Fillmore suffered severe damage during the Loma Prieta disaster and was demolished.

BIRD'S-EYE VIEW OF
GOLDEN GATE PARK
SAN FRANCISCO, 1892.

Chasing the Sunset

To many mid-19th century San Franciscans, the dream of developing an impressive public park in what was then a dreary, windy, sand dune–infested quarter known as the "Outside Lands"—pretty much everything from modern-day Divisadero Street west to the Pacific— seemed nothing short of ludicrous. No less an authority than Frederick Law Olmsted, the onetime superintendent of New York City's Central Park and Victorian America's foremost landscape architect, rejected the proposal. He recommended instead that the city create a greenbelt stretching from Hayes Valley, north along Market Street and Van Ness Avenue, to Aquatic Park. Local officials were less than enthusiastic.

Fortunately, William Hammond Hall was not nearly as skeptical. A former army surveyor, he won the bid in 1870 to conduct a topographical survey of the Outside Lands. A year later, he was appointed the first superintendent of the proposed Golden Gate Park. Hall began by planting a block-wide strip of realty known as the Panhandle, squeezed between Fell and Oak streets in the Haight-Ashbury on the park's eastern end. People who were looking for speedy progress were disappointed; Hall experimented with barley and sea bent grass to immobilize the shifting sand, and then he got to the business of spreading topsoil and manure.

In addition to his battle with nature, he also had to combat critics who thought the whole 1,017 acres set aside for this park should be flattened, with the excess earth to be used as fill in other parts of the city. Hall insisted that the property's natural features should be retained as much as possible.

A NEW SPIRIT

Despite Hall's successes, he was finally forced from office in 1876, with political detractors casting his earth-shaping campaign as a boondoggle of historic proportions. It took another decade before he was able to win that office back—and then one of the first and most promising things he did was hire a successor. Which is how eccentric Scottish landscaper John McLaren became the driving spirit of Golden Gate Park.

McLaren, who had studied horticulture at the Royal Botanical Gardens in Edinburgh and worked on land reclamation projects along the North Sea coast before moving to California, was strong-willed,

Nurses from the Veteran's Hospital at Fort Miley cool off by taking a dip in the Pacific near Seal Rocks on a hot day in 1949.

Left: An 1892 artist's rendering of a bird's-eye view of Golden Gate Park

Laughing Sal, the former face of Playland at the Beach, now resides in the Musée Mécanique at Fisherman's Wharf.

A ticket from the *San Francisco Chronicle's* "Children's Day" at the 1894 California Midwinter International Exposition at Golden Gate Park

given to liberal and inventive cursing, and particularly adept at making enemies in the municipal bureaucracy. But from the time he took the superintendent's reins in 1890 until his death in 1943, McLaren dreamed of turning Golden Gate Park into an environmental showplace. He fought excessive road-building through his parkland and resisted the mounting of the 1894 California Midwinter International Exposition on its east end. And while he could not forbid them entirely, he concealed in shrubbery the numerous statues that politicians and other do-gooders kept erecting in this green oasis. When asked in 1936 on his 90th birthday what he most wanted for a gift, "Uncle John," as generations of San Franciscans had come to know him, had a simple answer: "10,000 yards of good manure"—plenty of fertilizer for his beloved gardens.

LOFTY DREAMS

Today, Golden Gate Park is one of the finest green spaces in the nation. It is particularly pleasant on Sundays, when cars are forbidden and the roads are given over to skaters, runners, and bicyclists. And it's John McLaren, in large part, whom we have to thank for it.

While Uncle John had his hands in the dirt, Adolph Sutro had his head in the clouds. After making millions from Nevada's Comstock Lode, he enhanced

his fortune with real estate, buying up sandy lots and then selling them at a profit as the town expanded westward. Sutro spent much of his fortune collecting books (by the time of his death, it's said he owned the world's largest private library) and popularizing the city's Pacific shoreline. He took what had been a modest entertainment facility at Point Lobos, the Cliff House, and turned it into a baronial castle, hosting U.S. presidents and anyone else who could afford the nickel streetcar fare to its doorstep. Adjacent to that he built a complex of fancy public baths that might have dwarfed any such facilities ancient Rome had to offer.

CONEY ISLAND WEST

Hoping to build on Sutro's ventures, in the early 20th century an entrepreneur named George Whitney took over and expanded an amusement park just south of the Cliff House, promisingly named Playland at the Beach. Like Neptune Beach in Alameda, on the east side of San Francisco Bay, Playland fancied itself the West Coast's answer to Coney Island. And for a while, Whitney prospered, even buying the shrunken Cliff House that had replaced Sutro's palace. But in the end, Playland disappeared, too, leaving behind little more than a hand-carved carousel (now operating at Yerba Buena Gardens south of Market) and Laughing Sal, a mirthful mechanical character that today greets visitors at the Musée Mécanique, a storehouse of penny arcade games at Fisherman's Wharf.

Some dreams, it seems, are just too big.

An aerial view of Golden Gate Park shows just how expansive this greensward really is.

GOLDEN GATE PARK

By 1878, superintendent William Hammond Hall had supervised the construction of two miles of roads and bridal paths through embryonic Golden Gate Park, and more than 135,000 shrubs and trees were already in the ground. People who had questioned the efficacy of developing this giant common were amazed by its quick acceptance. According to one news report, in 1886 more than 50,000 people a day (or 20 percent of San Francisco's population at the time) visited the park, most of them traveling by streetcar. They came to picnic or to wander around the lakes and artificial waterfalls. Others arrived hoping to see the domed Conservatory of Flowers, which was modeled after one in London's Kew Gardens. This structure of glass, wood, and iron (above, in 1897) had been ordered from a Dublin designer by millionaire hotelier James Lick, who had intended it for his own San Jose estate. But Lick died in 1876, before it could be unpacked. His trustees put the structure on the market, and a contingent of wealthy locals, including Leland Stanford, purchased it and gave it to the park. The oldest building on the grounds, it was erected here in 1878.

De Young Museum

An art museum has flanked the park's Music Concourse ever since 1894, when an Egyptian temple-like Fine and Decorative Arts Building was constructed as part of the Midwinter Fair. After the exposition closed, it became the Midwinter Memorial Museum, with an art collection donated in large part by *San Francisco Chronicle* publisher Michael H. de Young. Though damaged by the 1906 quake, the museum held on until 1929, when it was finally demolished. Meanwhile, de Young commissioned architect Louis Mullgardt (who had contributed to the 1915 Panama-Pacific Expo) to create a new, Spanish Plateresque–style facility just to the west. That pink and white M. H. de Young Memorial Museum (above, in the 1920s or '30s) was completed in 1926, but it was later stripped of its increasingly unstable decorative elements. Undermined by the 1989 Loma Prieta earthquake, the museum closed in 2000 and was replaced by a new de Young in the same location, created by Swiss architects Jacques Herzog and Pierre de Meuron. Copper clad, with a twisting, 144-foot-tall observation tower, it opened in 2005.

Bicycle Craze

The 1890s marked the height of America's bicycle craze, and San Francisco was not immune. Despite condemnation by clergy, who remonstrated against bike riding as an invitation to sin (since it gave women freedom to travel and let couples escape the overprotective gaze of their elders), on pleasant days fitness-conscious locals could be spotted wobbling all over town on new-style "safety bicycles." However, streetcar and cable car "slots," as well as inadequately maintained roadways, made this sport dangerous in some places. Easier to tackle were the even pathways veining Golden Gate Park. The pair of cyclists shown above, with their baby strapped into a novel frame between them, was shot in 1890. *Top:* The bicycle craze continues in this green space today.

JAPANESE TEA GARDEN

A tranquil combination of bridges, footpaths, shrines, pools, and bonsai trees, the Japanese Tea Garden is one of the park's favorite attractions. Originally called the Japanese Village, it began as a Midwinter Fair concession, run by Australian George Turner Marsh, who imported Asian art and once operated a Japanese art gallery in the Palace Hotel. On his Marin County estate, Marsh had an extensive Japanese garden and employed several Japanese families, who he shipped over to build the fair's village, along with a two-story gate—a replica of which now stands at the garden's main entrance. (Another gate to the south came from the 1915 Panama-Pacific International Exposition.) After the fair closed, Marsh sold his concession to the park, and in 1895 Japanese landscaper Makoto Hagiwara was hired to manage the grounds and the teahouse. The Hagiwaras kept at those tasks and expanded the garden from one acre to five until World War II, when they and other Japanese Americans were sent to detention camps. The site was briefly renamed the Oriental Tea Garden and lost some of its plantings and features, but it has since been given a second life.

A few finely dressed strollers take in the sights at the Japanese Tea Garden, circa 1900.

Dutch Windmills

Among the distinctive sights on the extreme western end of Golden Gate Park are two Dutch windmills, erected in the early 20th century to help pump fresh groundwater for use on John McLaren's thirsty gardens. These romantic-looking contraptions once provided up to 100,000 gallons of water every hour. Electric pumps were installed later, stealing the windmills' purpose. The north windmill, originally built in 1902 (and shown at left), was restored and rechristened in 1981 and is surrounded by a tulip garden—the gift of Queen Wilhelmina of the Netherlands. Murphy's Windmill to the south (above, in the early 1900s), named for banker Samuel Murphy, who donated it to the city in 1905, is still in the process of restoration.

MEET ME AT THE FAIR

OVER THE OBJECTIONS of John McLaren, San Francisco's first world's fair, the California Midwinter International Exposition, opened on 200 acres at Golden Gate Park's eastern end on January 27, 1894. Its mastermind was Michael H. de Young, the publisher and cofounder (with

The Grand Court and Administration Building

his brother, Charles) of the *San Francisco Chronicle*. He'd taken charge of California's exhibits at the 1893 World's Columbian Exposition in Chicago and returned home full of ideas for a smaller spectacle here. Though staged quickly, this so-called Midwinter Fair proved impressive. Most of the major buildings were designed with Egyptian or Indian flair, and they were grouped around a central Grand Court. All of California's counties, a number of U.S. states, and three dozen foreign nations were represented. A 260-foot Tower of Electricity rose from the fairground's middle and at night trained its searchlight over the surrounding city. Exotic attractions included a South Sea Island village, where cannibal dances were staged; a Japanese village in which patrons tasted the very first fortune cookies served in the United States; and an Esquimaux (Eskimo) village complete with a pond where native Alaskans paddled around in skin-covered kayaks. By the time its gates closed on July 9, the fair's attendance was recorded as 2,255,551—roughly seven times the city's population. McLaren subsequently demolished most of de Young's exposition, save for the Egyptian-style Fine and Decorative Arts Building, the Grand Court (which became the Music Concourse), and the Japanese Tea Garden.

CLIFF HOUSE

Point Lobos, named by Spanish explorers for the sea lions (*lobos marinos,* or sea wolves) that languished and barked on the surrounding rocks, is the westernmost tip of San Francisco. It's been a leisure destination since the mid-1850s. In 1863, a real-estate speculator named Charles Butler constructed the first fairly modest Cliff House just south of that point. It initially attracted the chic and well-heeled set, who ventured out by carriage over a toll road (later Geary Boulevard) to dawdle and dine, to survey the marine life on adjacent Seal Rocks, or to thrill at the sight of daredevils treading tightropes above the crashing waves. However, as more common folk discovered this resort and competitors for the coastal tourist trade appeared, Butler added card rooms and saloons to the Cliff House, both of which lent it an unsavory reputation.

A crowded Cliff House hosted sightseers, socialites, and diners in 1866.

In the early 1880s, Adolph Sutro purchased the Cliff House. A Prussian-born entrepreneur and resolute dreamer, he had made a fortune in Nevada's Comstock mining country. After acquiring an idyllic cottage on the promontory above the Cliff House and Seal Rocks, which he enlarged and surrounded with gardens full of scandalously underdressed statues, Sutro began restoring the respectability of Butler's former oceanside resort. Although a chimney fire burned the Cliff House to the ground in 1894, Sutro seemed undiscouraged. With architects Emile S. Lemme and C. J. Colley, he soon erected a grander, French château–style replacement, stuffed with private dining rooms, curio shops, and parlors (top, circa 1900). He also built an electric trolley line out to the beach so more people of lesser means could enjoy his entertainments.

The Cliff House Today

Adolph Sutro died in 1898, setting off a years-long battle between his heirs for what he left behind. In 1907, his luxurious Cliff House went up in flames during a remodeling project *(left)*. It was replaced two years later by a conspicuously less grandiose (but more fire-resistant) version, the essence of which still stands today.

SUTRO BATHS

Beside the Cliff House on the north, the ambitious Sutro raised the largest public bathhouse in the world. Opened officially in 1896, while its creator was serving his first and only term as mayor of San Francisco, Sutro Baths boasted seven swimming pools (the largest being an unheated, L-shape seawater pool 300 feet long and 175 feet wide) and 500 dressing rooms. The Victorian structure, with its Greek temple-like entrance, was roofed by two acres of crystal glass and contained sweeping staircases, gardens of palms and ferns, restaurants, a theater, a gymnasium, and an eccentric museum that showcased Egyptian mummies, stuffed animals, medieval armor, and even a carnival made of toothpicks crafted by a penitentiary inmate. The palatial playland is pictured here, circa 1898.

Above: One of the immense swimming pools at the Sutro Baths, circa 1898. *Left:* A flyer for one of this sight's many public spectacles, which dates to the early 1900s.

The Sutro Baths persisted as a recreation center well into the 20th century, though its largest pool was turned into an ice-skating rink in 1937. Declining attendance and rising maintenance costs finally shuttered the facility in 1966, shortly after which it burned, leaving what some call "the finest ruins in the city." It is now part of the Golden Gate Recreation Area. Visitors today can climb the cliffs that once contained the mammoth waterfront attraction.

OCEAN BEACH

Cheap and easy transportation brought weekend crowds not only to the Cliff House, but also to six-mile-long Ocean Beach, immediately south of there. In the 1880s, a sizable concert and dance hall (on the lower left in the photo below), was erected to the north of Golden Gate Park. Over the next four decades, it was joined by a carousel (created by Charles I. D. Looff, who'd installed the first carousel at New York's Coney Island in 1876), a shooting gallery, and a Chutes-at-the-Beach water ride. In 1922, the now legendary wooden Big Dipper roller coaster, with its 3,000 feet of track and hair-raising drops, was built nearby. Thousands of San Franciscans came every summer to sample the concessions and dip their exhausted feet in the chilly Pacific surf. *Right:* Ocean-goers enjoy the sand and surf in the early 1900s.

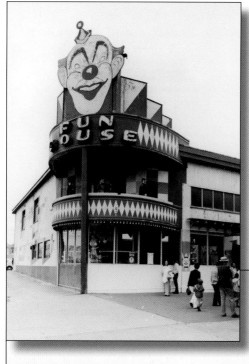

Playland Fun House

In the late 1920s, brothers George and Leo Whitney, who for years had operated quick-photo stands and shooting galleries at Ocean Beach, took over the management of this seaside entertainment complex and dubbed it Playland at the Beach. They added dozens of concessions and attractions, including a fun house, a Tilt-a-Whirl, a museum containing life-size murals of famous people, and Laughing Sal, an automated figure given to raucous and child-frightening guffaws. A combination fried chicken house and dance hall, Topsy's Roost, was a hot spot for adults, but younger patrons preferred their calories in the form of a Whitney invention, the It's-It ice-cream sandwich—two oatmeal cookies around a scoop of vanilla, all dipped in chocolate. Playland survived the Depression, only to fail before more modern competition in 1972 (shown at left the year it closed).

Around early spring and summer, Ocean Beach is almost always engulfed in San Francisco's typically foggy weather. Beach-goers relish in a walk along the sand on an uncharacteristically clear day.

WESTERN SUBURBS

While Mount Davidson at 938 feet is the tallest hill in San Francisco, Twin Peaks just to the north of there may be more widely recognized. (If only because on clear days you can spot it from downtown looking west along Market Street.) Native Americans believed that these two summits were once quarreling spouses whom the Great Spirit separated. The Spanish later identified the gracefully shaped and grassy cones on their maps as *Los Pechos de la Choca*, or "The Breasts of the Indian Maiden." Both summits rise to about 920 feet. Aside from a reservoir, modern communications towers, a two-mile-long streetcar tunnel that opened in 1918 and runs from the Castro to the West Portal neighborhood, and a scenic point on top that offers stunning views, Twin Peaks haven't changed since the photo above was taken from the Castro in 1901.

The Chutes

The closure of Woodward's Gardens in 1891 left San Franciscans hungry for new amusements. Enter the Chutes parks. The first of these sprang up in 1895 on Haight Street between Cole and Clayton. Its main attraction was Shoot-the-Chutes, a ride that sent people in boats careening at 60 miles an hour down a steep waterslide to splash into a lagoon. Over time that park added a roller coaster, zoo, and vaudeville house. It eventually outgrew its space, about the same time real-estate prices in the Haight-Ashbury drove it to new digs among the sand dunes of Richmond. The new park opened in 1902 on Fulton Street between 10th and 11th. All the original entertainments, including the Chutes ride (left, in the early 1900s), made the move and were joined by a movie theater and a Circle Swing that sent thrill-seekers in basket cars suspended by cables spinning around a central wheel. In 1909, the park moved to the Fillmore District, but after a fire two years later, it shut down for good.

Sunset and Richmond Districts

In the late 1800s, much of what are now the Sunset and Richmond districts were covered with sand dunes. No more than a few hundred people called Sunset home until after the 1906 quake—with some of them living in "Carville-by-the-Sea," an area adjacent to Ocean Beach that was filled with retired horse-drawn streetcars converted into small family residences. But as real-estate speculators learned the means to stabilize the dunes and turn them into buildable land, houses sprang up all over the western edge of town. By the late 1920s, there were some 30,000 people living in the Sunset, and that number climbed to 48,000 by 1940, around when this photograph was taken. The last major sand dune is said to have disappeared in the '70s. Today, there's hardly any undeveloped land left in the district.

PALACE OF THE LEGION OF HONOR

Alma de Bretteville Spreckels, born in the Sunset District in 1881, cut a wide swath through early-20th century San Francisco. An artist's model turned arts patron, she married the much older Adolph Spreckels in 1908. He was the son of sugar tycoon Claus Spreckels. With his millions, she built a Pacific Heights mansion. Then, during a furniture and art shopping excursion to Europe, she met French sculptor Auguste Rodin and subsequently persuaded Adolph to finance construction of a new art museum at Lincoln Park, in the city's far northwest corner. Together with architect George Applegarth, who had also designed her stately home, "Big Alma" built what was more or less a copy of the French Pavilion from the 1915 Panama-Pacific International Exposition, which had itself been modeled after Paris's Palais de la Légion d'Honneur. Construction of the museum began in 1921 *(left)*, and it opened in 1924, only months after Adolph Spreckels's demise.

Lands End

Tyrannized by high winds, sculpted by waves, and notorious as the site of many a shipwreck, the headlands of Lands End—west of the Golden Gate and down the hill from the Palace of the Legion of Honor—are known as San Francisco's wildest bit of coastline. The 1941 photo at right shows what remains of the residence of unofficial Lands End "mayor" Charles Harris; the building was wrecked by slides, floods, and termites. The structure to the right was a refreshment stand where, for more than three decades, hikers and sightseers visiting the area could stop on their way out to the vista point. Today's explorers can hike scenic coastal trails from Sutro Baths, south of here, to Fort Point and the Golden Gate Bridge to the north.

Now managed by the city, together with Golden Gate Park's M. H. de Young Museum, the California Palace of the Legion of Honor showcases the Spreckels's collection of Rodin sculptures *(right)* as well as paintings, drawings, and decorative works that illustrate 4,000 years of ancient and European art.

HONNEUR ET PATRIE

Index